This book belongs to:

This book is dedicated to Jonah. Thank you for reading the books – love LIZ ♡ xx
Hello, Pichon Class and Mr Thompson!
To Toby and Zoe
Hello to Mika
Go Team Scholastic!
Thank you to Lyn and Jason!
Thank you to Lauren, Wendy, Andrew and Olivia

TOM GATES
IS
HA! HA!
HILARIOUS

By Liz Pichon
(who is also hilarious!)

SCHOLASTIC

First published in the UK by Scholastic, 2024
This edition published 2025
Scholastic, Bosworth Avenue, Warwick, CV34 6UQ
Scholastic Ireland, 89E Lagan Road, Dublin Industrial Estate,
Glasnevin, Dublin, D11 HP5F

ISBN 978-93-5954-087-0

A CIP catalogue record for this book is available from the British Library.

www.scholastic.co.uk

For safety or quality concerns:
UK: www.scholastic.co.uk/productinformation
EU: www.scholastic.ie/productinformation

This reprint edition: November 2025

Printed in India at Acme Print O Pac. Pvt.Ltd. Noida.

ANTS IN PANTS
It's about ANTS IN PANTS and Chocolate Spread
Featuring Grumpy ANT

ANTS IN PANTS
Grumpy Ant
This is mine!
Choco Spread
Hands off.
Chocolate Spread
No one eat it OR ELSE.
I'm off to be grumpy...
Yum
Choco Spread
I'll get my friends...
Hey! Come on up!
There's a treat.
We're coming!

Choco Spread
Eat up!
Choco Spread
Choco Spread
EMPTY
Choco Spread
It's gone!
Where?
To a good place!
Yum!

I'm getting ready for school when I remember I ~~want~~ HAVE to take the **COMIC** I've been making with me. But I can't find it

It's not in my bedroom.

Or my school bag.

I can't see it under ANY of the

cushions.

I even check behind the coats...

Nope, not there.

It's not in the laundry basket ...

or

under the cereal box.

What are you doing under the table, Tom?
Mum wants to know.
POPS
Looking for the comic I made...
I explain, and I crawl back out.
You don't want to be late for school.
I've GOT to find it though!
I tell Mum.
Is it for a school project then?
she asks.
I WISH! I promised Derek I'd show him my comic.
It'll turn up ... and you've got chocolate spread on your face, Tom.
Oh.
I use my sleeve to wipe it off.
I can tell Mum's not taking my missing comic SERIOUSLY.

"Don't wipe the chocolate off your face like THAT!" Mum says (a bit too late).

"But what about my **COMIC?** I need to take it with me!" I tell Mum again.

"Is THIS what you're looking for, Tom?"

It's Delia and she's HOLDING my **COMIC.**

I shout, and try to GRAB it.

Delia enjoys LIFTING it out of my reach so I can't get it.

"Did you help yourself to my chocolate spread, Tom? The one I bought for myself, so you wouldn't stick your fingers in it or LICK the spoon and put it back?"

Delia asks me.

(It's like she knows me...)

I ignore her question and say, "HEY, that's mine!" She's STILL got my **comic** and I can't reach it, even when I jump up.

"Just like the CHOCOLATE SPREAD is MINE, Tom. Stop eating it AND stop drawing me in your **COMICS!**"

Delia says CROSSLY, so I point out...

"I didn't draw YOU - I drew an ANT."

Mum steps in and takes my **comic.**

"Enough, you two...

Tom, go and do your teeth, then you can have it back," she says, then she turns to Delia.

"I'm SURE Tom didn't know it was your chocolate spread."

"Exactly," I add.

"I'm SURE he did. Don't help yourself next time."

It's not like I ate THAT much.

OK...

When I come back downstairs, Mum's been reading my **comic** and she says,

"Tom, this is **HILARIOUS!** I love it! I can tell where you get your ideas from, but maybe don't put your teachers OR your parents in your **COMICS!**"

"Too late – Tom's drawn one with you and Dad dancing BADLY," Delia decides to tell Mum.

(How does Delia know about my other **comics?**

She MUST have been SNOOPING in MY room.)

Before I go to school, Mum gives me back my **comic.**

"It's great, Tom, well done - now, don't be late as Derek's waiting for you."

"Thanks, Mum," I say, and smile at Delia, like the FAVOURITE child.

"HEY, TOM!" Delia calls me back. "Don't forget your packed lunch... It's DELICIOUS."

Then she hands over my packed lunch.

(How does she know it's delicious?)

I head off to meet Derek and try not to think about what Delia **might** have done to my lunch...

EMPTY

"Nothing, I hope.

Derek's waiting outside and says,

"I've got a joke for you, Tom."

Which is a good start to the day.

"How did the  octopus make the fish LAUGH?"

"With a hilarious joke?" I say.

"Not quite... It made the fish laugh with ... ten tickles. Get it?"

(It takes me a while...)

"Do you want to know what else is FUNNY?" I ask him.

"This..." Derek says, and he pulls a silly face.

I laugh more when he stops.

"No – THIS. My **comic.** I drew Delia as an ANT who likes CHOCOLATE SPREAD."

"Who doesn't? You had some this morning," Derek says.

"How do you know?"

"It's on your face."

"Oh ... still?"

"I'll read it at break time, Tom – I can't read and WALK at the same time."

(Good point.)

Derek and I spend the rest of the walk to school thinking of different things I could get the ANTS IN PANTS to do in my **comics.**

We get to school on time and notice a BIG group of kids all STARING at something.

"What's going on? Let's go over and see," Derek says – so we walk over.

It's a little kid that I don't recognize who's drawing in chalk all over the ground...

"Hey, Tom. That looks like your drawings!" Derek points out.

I'm thinking the EXACT same thing, when I hear someone say:

"WOW! She's SO good at drawing. That's AMAZING – and FUNNY too!"

It's Marcus Meldrew.

Other kids start agreeing with him.

"Look, Tom – she can draw aliens and funny fish," says Marcus.

"I can draw aliens and funny fish too. And ants and all kinds of stuff," I remind Marcus and anyone else who can HEAR me.

"I like your drawings, Tom," says Derek.

"Thanks, Derek."

"But she is really good, isn't she?" he adds.

The bell goes for the start of school, so we go inside.

"See you at break time, Derek, with my HILARIOUS **comics** that I DREW," I tell Derek in a LOUD voice.

"Can't wait," Derek says.

On the way to class, I overhear more kids chatting about the AMAZING drawings the little kid was doing.

"I've never seen drawings as good or as FUNNY as that," someone says.

I HAVE.

I say, but no one takes any notice.

In class, I take out my **COMIC** and show it to **AMY**.

She'll like it, I'm sure.

"Do you want to read my **COMIC?** I drew it myself. It's HILARIOUS!"

Marcus *LEANS* over.

"Is it though ... REALLY?"

"I'll read it later, Tom. Mr Fullerman's here and we've got assembly. AND did you see that little kid's drawing? It was good, wasn't it?" **AMY** asks.

"They were OK – they looked like MY drawings," I say.

"Like yours ... but better!" Marcus interrupts.

"You haven't seen my Ants In Pants," I point out, and WAVE my **comic** around.

"Let's see it then," Marcus says.

"Later – AMY'S reading it first and then Derek," I let him know.

"Fine... I'm going to make my own comic and keep a journal FULL of funny stories and things I see," Marcus tells us proudly.

"You should do it," I say. "**Comics** take a long time to draw and write. I try and make MY **comics** HILARIOUS so anyone who reads them will laugh NON-STOP."

Marcus smiles. "I WILL. I've got loads of ideas and A LOT of things to SAY."

AMY sighs. "Yes, we know."

Mr Fullerman takes the register and then leads us to the school hall. He stands at the front of the hall, ready to take today's assembly.

When Mrs Nap starts playing the piano, he gets a bit of a *SHOCK.*

(We all do.)

Her arms are moving up and down SO fast they're a **BLUR**.

Normally Mrs Nap plays something slow and calming. But this tune is EXTRA LOUD and "**JOLLY**".

We all start clapping along to her playing, which makes some kids think it's a **school disco** and they start dancing.

One kid does a handstand ...

... that doesn't end well.

AGH!

CLONK!

Mr Fullerman is forced to do one of his **BIG beady-eyed STARES.**

Everyone (including Mrs Nap) STOPS.

The hall goes VERY QUIET, apart from the kid who fell over, who is going...

"Awwwwwwwwww!"

"WELL, THAT was a lively start to our day!"

What A LOT of energy you all have this morning!

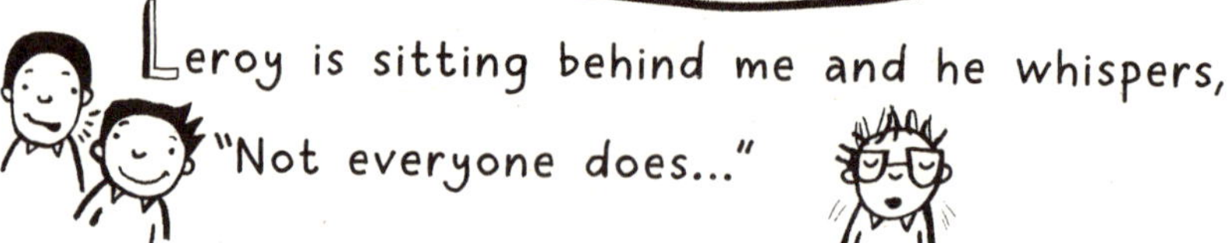

Leroy is sitting behind me and he whispers, "Not everyone does..."

We can both see Norman, who's got his eyes closed.

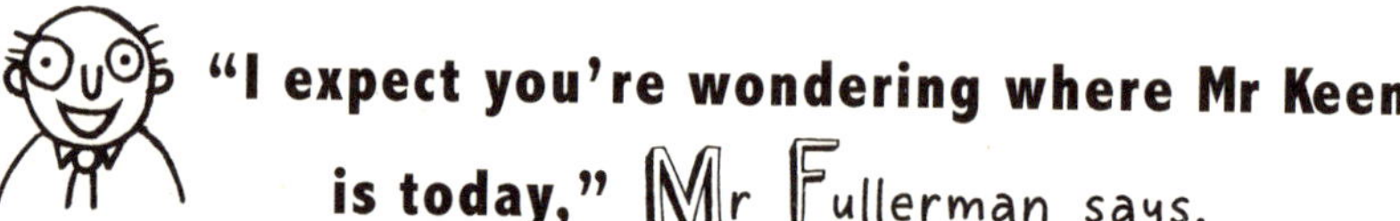

"I expect you're wondering where Mr Keen is today," Mr Fullerman says.

"Not really..." I whisper, and make Leroy and AMY LAUGH.

"Mr Keen is taking some time off school with a SPORTS injury.

We wish him a *SPEEDY* RECOVERY and hope he gets well and comes back soon,"

Mr Fullerman explains.

"In the meantime, we have a NEW member of staff, who'll be covering my lessons while I step into Mr Keen's VERY LARGE and important shoes."

"We've got a supply teacher?" I say, looking around the hall.

"Why is Mr Fullerman wearing Mr Keen's shoes?" Marcus wonders.

"He's not," AMY says.

Mr Fullerman continues to build up the introduction...

"Let's give a BIG OAKFIELD SCHOOL WELCOME to ...

Miss Jam!"

Miss Jam waves at us and smiles.

HELLO, EVERYONE!

"It's lovely to be here. I'm just sorry that Mr Keen hurt his back. And before anyone asks ... my FIRST name is not Strawberry or Traffic. I've heard EVERY JOKE going – so don't even try," she tells us.

(This feels like a challenge.)

"She seems nice," AMY says.

"Wait until she's in the classroom – sometimes teachers change," Leroy whispers.

He's got a point. It can happen.

Mr Fullerman looks like he's enjoying taking assembly, along with Mrs Nap, who asks us to sing a song.

There's no more WILD dancing, just singing.

At the end of the song, Mr Fullerman says:

"Thank you, Mrs Nap. Now, does anyone know who did the CHALK drawing in the playground?"

(WHAT? Is Mr Fullerman talking about the little kid's drawings NOW?)

Huh?

Someone calls out from the back of the hall:

"It was Tina... She's HERE!"

(Maybe she's in TROUBLE!)

We all look round at Tina, who doesn't seem that worried at all.

"It was lovely to see such creativity – well done, Tina!" Mr Fullerman says.

Tina stands up and starts WAVING like she's a FILM STAR.

This seems a little over the top, if you ask me.

"Whenever I draw on the playground, I just get told off!" I grumble.

AMY turns to me and says, "You have to admit, Tom, her drawing WAS—"

LIKE MINE?

I snap, as this is getting annoying.

Her drawings are FUNNY!

Marcus adds, though no one asked for his opinion.

"I'm just saying that Mr Fullerman's never congratulated me on my drawings," I mutter, but no one's taking much notice of me now. I spot Derek, who's sitting with his class, and try to get his ATTENTION.

He sees me, then starts trying to make me "LAUGH" by doing his impression of a turtle.

(It's a classic and it works.)

I wish Derek was in my class – although I might not get as much work done if he was.

Mr Sprocket wags his finger in Derek's direction to make him STOP!

He doesn't notice that I'm doing my turtle impression, and I stay like that until the end of assembly.

(It's quite cosy.)

Mr Fullerman reminds our class that we're going back with Miss Jam.

He also says he's going to miss teaching our class but knows we'll work hard and behave well. He's not sure WHEN Mr Keen will be coming back – but he doesn't think it'll be long. Then he heads off to Mr Keen's office, whistling happily.

Back in class, I've got so many ideas for my NEW **COMICS** that I start drawing in my notebook STRAIGHT AWAY.

IDEAS like this

Marcus decides to get out his notebook and begins writing and LAUGHING LOUDLY.

"What's so funny, Marcus?" AMY asks.

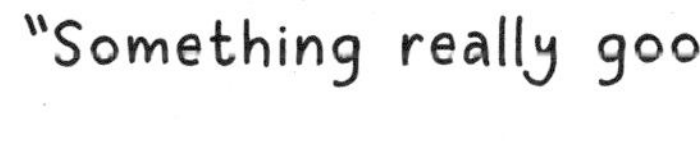

"Something really good."

"Let's see," I say.

"No - you might COPY me," Marcus tells me, and SHUTS his notebook.

"More like YOU might copy ME! And you wouldn't be the first!" I say.

Miss Jam is standing RIGHT by our table, waiting to start our first lesson. So we stop talking.

Usually the first lesson is **ART**.

But with Miss Jam being NEW, she might teach us something else.

I CLOSE my eyes and try WISHING for my favourite lesson.

Art, art, art...

What are you doing?

Marcus asks.

"Wishing for Miss Jam to say those THREE MAGIC WORDS..."

SPELLING TEST NOW?

Marcus thinks he's funny.

"No, I'm wishing for ...

Art Lesson Now!

Wish Wish
Wish Wish
Wish Wish

(Wishing doesn't always work, but it's worth a try.)

Wish Wish

Please rain. Please rain. Miss PE.

Oh.

Wish Wish

Cake and custard for pudding...

Oh.

Rice pudding.

I keep wishing as Miss Jam makes herself comfy at Mr Fullerman's desk. Then she gets straight to the point.

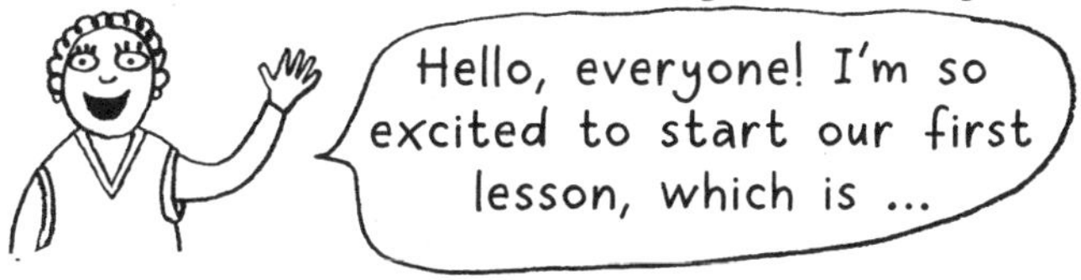

Hello, everyone! I'm so excited to start our first lesson, which is ...

Art, art, art...

... SCIENCE!

(Oh.)

I love science.

Sigh.

Bad luck, Tom.

Miss Jam tells us more.

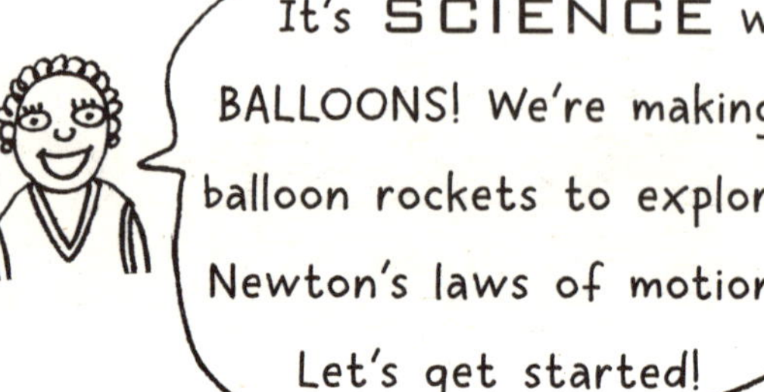

I take it back! I **WANT** to make a

BALLOON ROCKET!

This could be a good lesson after all.

Marcus enjoys reminding me.

Miss Jam has a huge selection of balloons, ready to blow up and use for the ROCKETS.

It makes the whole class feel like we're having a

This lesson is **ACE** and **Miss Jam** makes us **LAUGH** - she's SO nice.

I haven't enjoyed myself so much in a science lesson since we watched **Mr Fullerman** making a volcano in a sandpit.

My entire class is having the BEST time.

Mr Fullerman

Marcus insists on blowing up his OWN balloon.

I try telling him to STOP before it bursts...

But he won't listen ...

... until it's TOO LATE.

BANG

(I will put THAT in a comic for sure.)

I burst the balloon.

We ALL love making BALLOON ROCKETS.

Miss Jam is busy teaching and has her back to the door, so she doesn't see Mr Fullerman walk past our classroom and take a SNEAKY peek.

He can see we're having a GREAT lesson. (We are.)

Mr Fullerman seemed to be very happy about filling in for Mr Keen and NOT being our teacher for a while.

I'm SURE he won't miss us at all.

At break time, everyone is still BUZZING with EXCITEMENT after making BALLOON ROCKETS, especially Norman.

Look! I'm a rocket!

I can't wait to find Derek to show him my comic and tell him about the FUN lesson we've just had.

I SPOT him standing with a group of kids, looking at a wall...

Oh... It's Tina and she's drawing again.

"Hey, Tom. Come and see this," Derek says, with his eyes FIXED on the drawing.

So I do.

"It's like watching someone do MAGIC!" Derek tells me.

"Is it?" I'm not convinced at all.

"How did you get so good at drawing?" one girl asks Tina.

"I just love drawing. I do it as much as I can," Tina tells her.

"I love drawing too," I whisper to Derek. "It's no big deal really, is it? I mean, what's all the fuss about?" I add.

"You should look round the corner," he tells me. So I do.

"WHEN DID THAT HAPPEN? We've only been at break time for FIVE MINUTES! How's she drawn spaceships, aliens and all the other things that look like my drawing so FAST?" I grumble.

No one is listening as they're all watching Tina draw.

Derek says.

"It's OK. Do you want to read my **comic** now?"

I ask, trying to get his attention.

"Sure! Oh, wait – she's drawing a BIRD. I've always wanted to know how to draw a bird."

THIS is NEWS to me! "I can show you how to draw anything you want!"

I say this loudly enough that kids turn round and look at me like I'm spoiling Tina's concentration.

"Let's go over to the bench – you can read my **comic** there," I suggest.

"Fine..." Derek drags himself away.

I hand him the **comic** and wait for him to read it.

"Is that Delia?" he asks.

"Maybe..."

"I LOVE IT!" Derek LAUGHS.

(THIS is a good sign.) Then someone starts LAUGHING right in front of us. It's MARCUS. He's making NOTES in his journal like he's a REPORTER.

Ha! Ha!

"Everything OK, Marcus?" Derek asks him.

"Yes, thanks. I just need to finish my drawing."

Marcus smiles at us, makes a few more notes, then walks off, still LAUGHING.

"He started doing that in class. He said he's going to make a **comic**," I tell Derek.

"About what?" Derek asks.

"US, I think. Every time I look up, Marcus is THERE with his notebook."

AMY, Florence and Indrani walk up to the bench.

"Hey, Tom – have you seen that girl's drawing of a space world? It's SOOOOOO, SOOOOO good!" Indrani says.

"Actually, I've been busy with my OWN drawings. Do you want to see them? They're HERE in MY **comic.**"

"It's a really good **comic.** SHORT but still good," says Derek helpfully.

"Thanks, Derek. I'll make the next one longer, I promise."

"Pass it over, then." Florence takes my **comic** and they all read it.

(Quickly.)

I wait to see if they **LAUGH**.

"Has your sister Delia seen this yet? Did she like it?" **AMY** asks.

"Of course. She's my **BIGGEST** fan!"

Derek looks surprised. "Is she?"

"No, Derek, but I won't let that stop me drawing more **comics**," I assure him.

"It's funny, Tom," Florence tells me.

"A bit short, but I like the Ants In Pants," Indrani adds.

"The ant looks like Delia," **AMY** says.

"I don't know WHAT you mean!" I smile.

"Maybe you should start to draw Ants in Pants on the walls next, like Tina does?" Derek suggests.

"Remember when you doodled Mr Fullerman?"*

AMY reminds me.

"You NEARLY got into trouble – that was FUNNY!"

She LAUGHS.

"Me getting into trouble or the drawing?"

I check.

"You nearly getting into trouble!"

(Amy makes everyone laugh...)

"What's your new teacher like?" Derek asks.

* See *Tom Gates: Spectacular School Trip (Really).*

"She seems nice and we made rocket balloons, which was fun. The lesson flew by and was really interesting," I tell Derek.

"Sounds like my kind of lesson. Mr Sprocket made balloon animals once – that was good."

"Mr Fullerman's lessons are usually good – but Miss Jam's are better. She's SO FUNNY and SUCH a good teacher. I think Miss Jam is the

!" I say ...

... just as Mr Fullerman APPEARS from NOWHERE and hears

EVERYTHING.

"It's great that you're enjoying Miss Jam's lessons so much, Tom," Mr Fullerman says.

"We all are, sir," AMY adds.

"I'm VERY happy to hear that," Mr Fullerman tells us.

He's holding a HUGE stack of heavy box files and doesn't look happy.

"We'd better go, sir," I say. "Miss Jam says we've got another really FUN lesson next, and none of us want to be late."

"Yes, of course. OFF you all go ...

AND REMEMBER..."

Mr Fullerman starts to say something, but the door closes behind me and I don't hear the rest.

Inside our class, we get a LOVELY SURPRISE as Miss Jam's been super BUSY during break time. There's a BRAND-NEW display up already, with some of our ROCKET BALLOONS, along with pictures on the walls, more BOOKS, colourful bunting and TWO signs. One that says:

and the other:

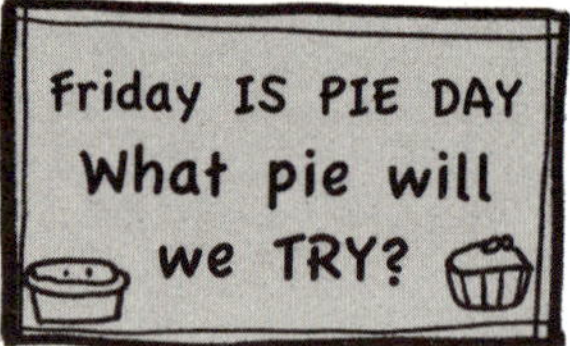

Welcome back, everyone!

Miss Jam says.

"Hurry up and sit down – I've got lots to share with you all."

Brad Galloway can't wait and SHOUTS from the back of the class:

Miss Jam, WHAT'S FRIDAY PIE DAY?

(It's what we're all wondering.)

"Miss Jam, who's **Rodney Rat?**"

Julia Morton wants to know...

"All good questions! Are you ready to meet..."

Miss Jam brings out a purple soft toy RAT from behind her back.

"**Rodney Rat,** everyone!"

"This is **Rodney Rat,** who LOVES to be read to. You'll all be able to bring **Rodney** home and take photos of the places you decide to READ YOUR BOOKS. But not on the toilet though – I don't want photos of THAT, thank you," Miss Jam tells us. Then straight away Brad Galloway says, "But that's my favourite place to read, miss!"

"Not with **Rodney,**" Miss Jam tells him, then she makes **Rodney** WAVE.

The whole class goes...

"Awwwwwwwww."

Apart from Trevor Peters, who puts his hand up. "What if you don't like rats, Miss Jam?"

"As long as you like READING, **Rodney** won't mind – will you, **Rodney?**"

Miss Jam pretends that **Rodney** is whispering to her.

"**Rodney** is also excited about FRIDAY PIE DAY! Would you like to know more about THAT?" she asks.

we all shout.

"There'll be a chance to try a different pie from different countries, with different ingredients – just because ... it's FUN!
We can record our favourite pies on the

!"

"Genius," I say to AMY.

"I'll be sending out permission slips. If anyone has allergies, ask your parents or caregivers to let me know."

"She's thought of everything," AMY whispers to me.

(TRUE).

"Friday Pie Day is all about discovering delicious NEW tastes ... and pies. I hope you're all looking forward to that!" Miss Jam says.

Normally I'd be suspicious about trying NEW food, but Miss Jam is making everything sound BRILLIANT and exciting and now I can't WAIT for FRIDAY.

The whole class feels the same way and starts to chant...

FRIDAY PIE DAY FRIDAY PIE DAY
FRIDAY PIE DAY FRIDAY PIE DAY

"Settle down, Class 5F ... or should I say 5J until Mr Fullerman comes back?" Miss Jam calls out.

(Makes sense to me.)

"Before we start our next lesson, we need to choose my HELPER OF THE DAY - who'll get EXTRA stars on Mr Fullerman's chart. Who'd like to pick out a name from this bag? How about ... YOU?"

Miss Jam says, and she's pointing at ME.

TODAY just gets BETTER! and BETTER!

I go to the front of the class, pick out a name, then hand it to Miss Jam.

"Thank you, Tom. Let's see who's going to be my special helper today. It's ..."

(Oh.)

Marcus jumps out of his chair like he's won a

He's happy to be chosen as HELPER OF THE DAY until Miss Jam asks him to

litter-pick at lunchtime

and suddenly he's NOT so happy.

BEFORE litter picking

AFTER litter picking

Marcus turns to me and says,

"Why did you pick my name?"

Like I did it on purpose!

"Think of the extra stars you'll get," I tell him.

(Amy laughs. Marcus doesn't.)

He cheers up when Miss Jam gives him a special HELPER sticker and asks him to hand out EXTRA pencils and worksheets.

Suddenly Marcus goes back to looking smug.

Even though I'm not GREAT at maths, Miss Jam makes the lesson FLY BY. She's so cheery and helpful ...

Miss Jam being cheery ...

... that I completely forget about Delia handing me my lunch box and saying my food was delicious ...

... until I open my lunch box and

find a

NOTE ...

... and inside it is a half-eaten biscuit.

My sister is HILARIOUS.

(NOT.)

But it doesn't stop me from eating the rest of the biscuit and drawing some of my own ants.

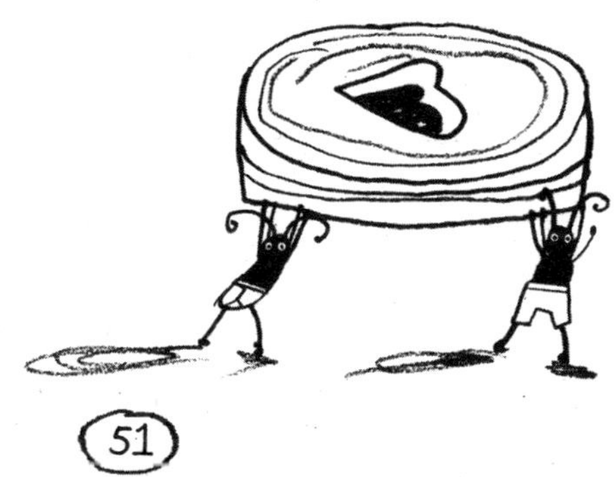

At lunch, Florence wants to share some **NEWS** about Mr Keen.

"I bet you can't GUESS why he's really off school," she says to us.

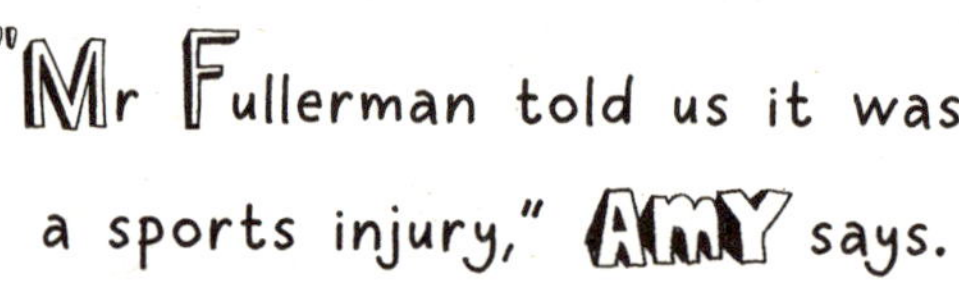

"Mr Fullerman told us it was a sports injury," AMY says.

"But <u>what</u> kind of SPORT was he doing?" Florence says.

(This gets us all thinking.)

"GOLF? I bet Mr Keen plays golf and hurt his back or got hit by a golf ball," I suggest.

Solid joins in. "Did he pull a muscle playing football?"

"Not even CLOSE! Keep guessing."

"He did a BUNGEE JUMP!"

Norman shouts.

Nearly! He was doing **CIRCUS SKILLS!**

I repeat.

None of us were expecting THAT.

Florence carries on telling her story. "I go to the sports centre to do **CIRCUS SKILLS** and juggling."

"Can you juggle, Florence?" AMY asks.

"Can you juggle these grapes?" Norman wants to know.

"I'm still learning – a bit like Mr Keen. He was in the ADULT **CIRCUS SKILLS** group and we share a hall. So I SPOT Mr Keen, which was a surprise – AND THEN I see that he's SITTING ON..."

"AN ELEPHANT!" Norman shouts.

(This story is going to take a long time to finish at this rate.)

"No, Norman... A **UNICYCLE.** Mr Keen was riding a **UNICYCLE,"** Florence repeats, so we can TAKE IN that information.

"At first Mr Keen is doing OK and I can see he's wobbling around, but SUDDENLY he loses control and does WONKY cycling all over the place."

Whoa...

(Florence is bringing this story to LIFE!)

"Then he cycles OUTSIDE, knocks over a tin of paint, and when he comes back..."

... he LEAVES a TRAIL OF **PAINT** EVERYWHERE HE CYCLES!

"I can't imagine Mr Keen on a **unicycle**." AMY LAUGHS.

"I can."

It's like Florence is writing the ANTS IN PANTS **comic** for me.

I take out my notebook and pen and do a quick ANTS IN PANTS doodle INSPIRED by Florence's excellent story!

"What happened NEXT?" Norman asks.

"Mr Keen makes the WORST MESS with paint and he's out of CONTROL **unicycling** all over the place until FINALLY he ..."

Florence SLAMS her hand down on the table.

"... FALLS OFF."

"No wonder Mr Keen didn't want anyone to know! Did he see YOU, Florence?" **AMY** asks.

"I don't think he saw anything – he was wobbling around so much."

"SPORTS INJURY sounds more DRAMATIC than **unicycle** paint disaster," Derek tells us.

"We're the ONLY kids in school who know what really happened to Mr Keen," Florence says. This is true.

I add a few more doodles to my notebook and show it to Florence.

"It's like you were there, Tom!"

"This is the start of a brand-new ANTS IN PANTS **comic!**" I say.

"Just don't let Mr Keen see it," AMY reminds me.

"It'll be OUR secret - no one will EVER know!" I say.

I keep drawing in class too – behind my school book so Miss Jam can't see me.

So far, so good.

FRONT

BACK

"You shouldn't be drawing in class, Tom. You'll get into trouble," Marcus tells me.

(Typical Marcus.)

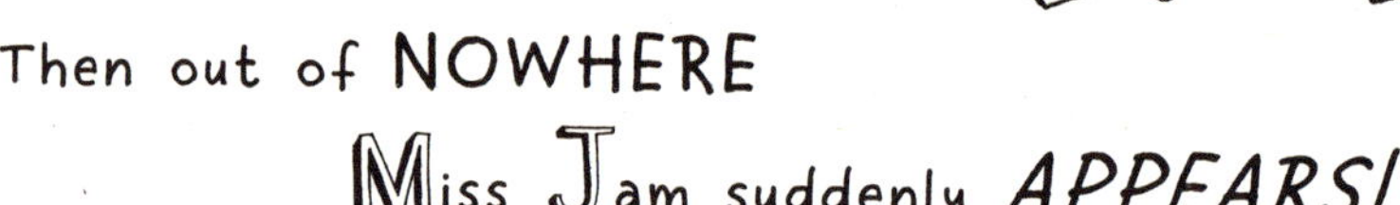

Then out of NOWHERE

Miss Jam suddenly *APPEARS!*

"HOW'S EVERYONE DOING?" she asks.

Marcus **LOOKS** like he's going to tell on me ... so I close my book FAST!

"GREAT, **M**iss **J**am! We really **LOVE** your lessons," I say.

"Thank you, Tom. Can you collect all the worksheets, please, Marcus?"

Miss **J**am keeps Marcus busy, and I'm all for it.

"Tom, do you have a worksheet or have you been busy doing something ELSE?" Marcus asks me.

I hand him a worksheet and smile.

(It's HIS worksheet - but I bet he won't realize it for a while.)

"Thank you, Marcus. Now, put up your hand if you'd like to take **Rodney Rat** home to read to," says Miss Jam.

OBVIOUSLY WE ALL DO!

Miss Jam looks around at all our hands in the air WAVING at her, then says:

"How about YOU at the BACK? Would you like to be first?"

It's Mark Clump, who for some reason says:

I LOVE SNAKES, mice, cats, dogs, all animals and RATS!

I can't WAIT until it's my turn to take **Rodney** home. Look at his cute RAT FACE.

Miss Jam has brought so much **Fun Stuff** into our lessons in such a short time.

she tells us, and I actually BELIEVE her!

When the bell goes for the end of school, Miss Jam asks us all to push our chairs in quietly.

(Like that's going to happen...)

Weirdly ... it does.

There's no chair noise at all.

Miss Jam is having a good effect on all of us.

SILENCE

(Mark Clump with **Rodney Rat** and a small suitcase.)

Derek is waiting for me right by Tina's wall doodle

... like I need reminding of that.

I want to show him the NEW **unicycle** comic I've been working on.

"It's called ...

ANTS IN PANTS **UNICYCLE Paint** Disaster!"

"Did you forget we've got band practice later?" he reminds me.

"NO - of course not."

(Yes - I'd forgotten...)

Mark Clump walks past us, holding **Rodney Rat**.

"That's **Rodney**," I let Derek know.

"Hey, Mark, where are you going to read with **Rodney** tonight?"

I ask him.

"Not sure – FIRST I have to feed my snake and lizard, clean out the bugs and spiders, and check the hedgehogs before I can read with **Rodney**."

"You need more pets, Mark!" Derek says.

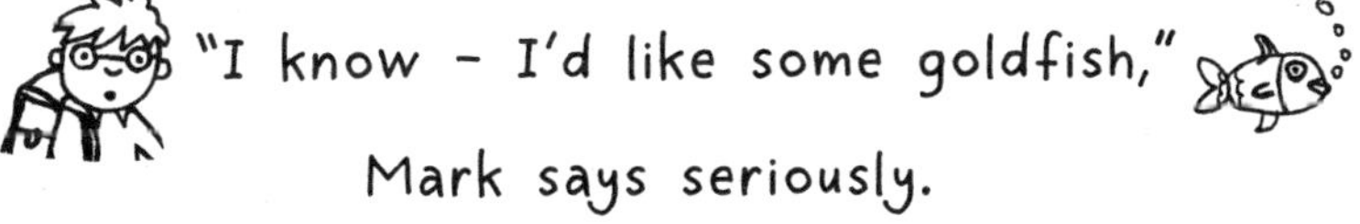

"I know – I'd like some goldfish," Mark says seriously.

"Or a hamster?" I add.

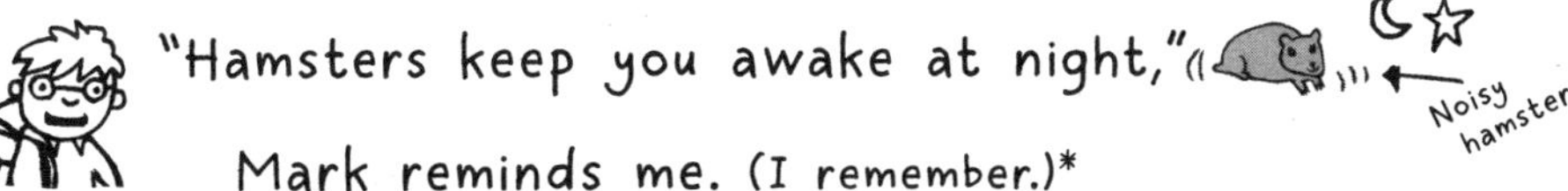

"Hamsters keep you awake at night," Mark reminds me. (I remember.)*

* See *Tom Gates: DogZombies Rule (For Now)* for hamster story.

On our walk home, I ask Derek which songs DOGZOMBIES should practise tonight.

"'Bicycle Race' by Queen," he answers quickly. It's a good shout.

"Or how about...

'I Can't Stand Up For Falling Down'*?" I suggest, and Derek likes that too.

We both try to think of more songs about bicycles or falling over...

but it's too hard.

"If we get time, let's write one of our OWN songs," Derek suggests.

"YES! We could write a song with ONE NOTE that will be easy to play and learn," I tell him.

"Good thinking, Tom," Derek agrees.

"That way we'll have more time for all the REALLY important things," he adds.

* This song is by Elvis Costello and the Attractions.

"Like practising..." I say.

"Like SNACKS," Derek says.

(TRUE.)

When I get home, I join Mum and Dad in the kitchen and am all ready to share

TODAY'S NEWS.

(There's A LOT...)

Mum's busy studying the fridge calendar, while Dad's stirring something on the cooker.

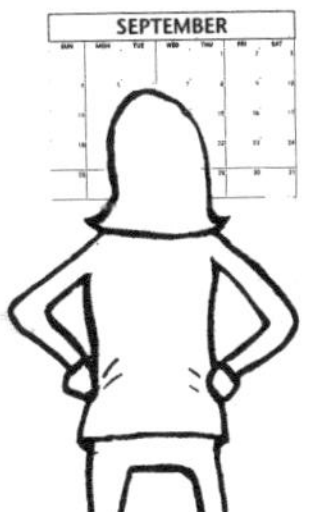

(Hopefully dinner.)

Nice cooking smells wafting

"Hi, Tom! Good day at school?"

Mum asks me.

And before I can answer, she points at the calendar and says, "Is that a FAMILY get-together at Uncle Kevin's this weekend?"

"I hope not... Hi, Tom – ready for some pasta?" says Dad.

"I've got BAND PRACTICE in an hour at Derek's, I have a **NEW COMIC** to finish AND some **NEWS** from school. We've got a new teacher called Miss Jam – her first name isn't STRAWBERRY or TRAFFIC."

I add this last part FAST as I know Dad will make a joke.

"What's happened to Mr Fullerman?" Mum wants to know.

"He's filling in for Mr Keen who fell off his **unicycle**," I explain.

"WHAT was Mr Keen doing on a **unicycle**?" Dad asks.

"Florence saw him at a **CIRCUS SKILLS** lesson. He lost control and **CYCLED** through some **paint,** then wobbled around and fell off. Mr Fullerman told EVERYONE in assembly he'd got a **sports injury**."

"Why was Mr Keen doing **CIRCUS SKILLS?"** Dad wonders.

"He's at that age, Frank, where he takes up hobbies and wears too much Lycra," Mum tells him.

"Dad wears LYCRA sometimes," I point out.

"EXACTLY!" Mum says.

"Hey - there's nothing wrong with Lycra. Come on, Tom, let's look at your **comic,"** Dad says, changing the subject.

"You've really got into **comics,** haven't you, Tom?" he adds.

(IT'S TRUE.)

"I like drawing FUNNY pictures,"

I say as Mum and Dad look at

"ANTS IN PANTS **UNICYCLE Paint** Disaster!"

Delia walks into the kitchen and sees that Mum and Dad are reading my latest **comic** <u>AND</u> they're smiling. ☺

"Is that ANOTHER **comic** about ME?" she asks.

"Not everything's about YOU, Delia."

She's holding her pot of chocolate spread AGAIN.

"I found <u>MY</u> chocolate spread in the garden with the lid OFF and it was EMPTY.

How did that happen ... TOM?"

"I don't know – it wasn't me.

Maybe some ANTS took it."

"Right – and I'll read about it in your next **comic.** You should REPLACE my chocolate spread,"

Delia tells me. (She's OBSESSED!)

"I'll get another pot," Mum sighs.

"It's just ANNOYING when Tom helps himself to MY things all the time!" Delia says, like I'm not stood right here.

"I didn't take your chocolate spread into the garden, Delia," I say again.

"I don't believe you, Tom," Delia whispers angrily.

It doesn't matter WHO finished it!

Mum's had enough, I can tell.

"Nice pasta, Frank," she adds.

"Thanks, Rita. I opened the jar myself." Dad smiles.

We all start eating and I let them know I might be bringing a friend home soon, called **Rodney**.

"**Rodney** is a RAT,"

I say, and watch Delia's face.

"YOU and **Rodney** can stay well away from me!" she says with a shudder.

"WHY are you bringing a rat home?

Is this like looking after a school pet?"

Mum asks.

"You do remember Delia's allergic to pets?"

Dad reminds me.

"But **Rodney Rat** is VERY well behaved."

(I'm enjoying pretending **Rodney's** a real rat.)

"When **Rodney's** here, I'm going to READ to him and take him to a **DOGZOMBIES** band practice."

"Why? What's the rat ever done to you?" Delia says.

"We've been practising a lot. We might even write a new song called 'The One Note Song'," I tell Delia.

"You should write a song called 'I Am a Chocolate Spread Thief'."

She is not giving up.

"I didn't take your chocolate spread – well, not ALL of it."

"I'm going to sing a song called 'HOLIDAY'!"

Mum sighs, then starts to sing it.

"Or you could sing 'Raindrops Keep Falling On My Head' and go camping,"

says Dad, joining in.

"Are we going camping?" I check.

(I'm guessing that's a no then.)

Delia gets up to leave.

"Thanks for dinner - but don't bring a rat home please, Tom."

(I will.)

I head off to Derek's for a quick band practice.

Turns out Leroy and Norman can't make it after all, so it's just me and Derek hanging out together ...

... mostly eating **Snacks.**

"Hey! I saw something **FUNNY** yesterday that I forgot to tell you," Derek says. "Your mum was in the garden holding a jar of chocolate spread and EATING

it with a spoon!"

MY MUM!

So she's the sneaky chocolate spread thief!

I say, **SHOCKED.** "Delia was blaming ME!"

"That sounds like Delia. Your mum looked like she was hiding. I watched your dad come out to the shed and she DUCKED behind a bush," Derek tells me.

"I can't believe it was Mum! She said she didn't like chocolate spread!"

"Are you going to say anything, Tom?"

Derek asks me.

"Not yet - I'll wait for the right moment. BUT that's another **GREAT** idea for a **comic.**"

"I want to read that right now!"

Derek tells me.

"We should really try and write a new song," I remind him.

"We should - that's why you came over."

"True..."

(Half an hour later.)

"Shall we watch TV?" Derek suggests.

"We should. Good idea."

(There's always time for The Jolly Fruit Bunch.)

When I get home, I keep the **NEWS** of Mum eating Delia's chocolate spread to myself (for now).

Instead, I FOCUS on doing some NEW drawings.

Then I **FINISH** the **comic** I started in school, as ALL my classmates are waiting to see it.

(Well, most of them.)

The title says it all...

Keen Ant
I have a NEW hobby!
Painting? Swimming? Something good for your back?
CIRCUS SKILLS.
I'm YOUNG!
You're not...!
CIRCUS SKILLS
I've GOT this!
Oh...
I can ride this unicycle.
Can you? It takes balance.
But I have good EYEBROWS.
Oh.
Easy, SEE!
I'm a natural.
Natural disaster.
Whatever you do, don't go outside.
I'm going OUTSIDE!
AGH!

Who put that there?
Sorry!
There's paint everywhere.
paint
Whose idea was this?
Yours!

Agh!
STOP that.
SORRY!
Do something, Keen Ant.
My EYEBROWS - I can't SEE!
Then one ant in pants had an IDEA to STOP Keen Ant.
Use this crash mat!
JUMP!

OK!
Keen Ant jumps towards the crash mat.
Oh no...
Ambulance, please.
OW!
Thud.
Thud.
What's that?
Your new hobby.
I'm cross.
CROSS WORDS

The next morning, Mr Fullerman is

waiting at the school gates, just like Mr Keen would normally do.

"Good morning, Tom and Derek."

"Morning, sir."

Mark Clump's here too.

He's holding **Rodney Rat** and making him WAVE at Mr Fullerman.

"Who's that, Mark? You know you're not supposed to bring TOYS into school," Mr Fullerman tells him.

"It's **Rodney Rat**, sir - he belongs to Miss Jam and she's letting us take him home. THEN we have to read aloud to **Rodney** anywhere BUT the toilet - that's not allowed," Mark explains.

"Miss Jam's got a toy rat? How interesting," Mr Fullerman says. (NOT sounding interested at all.)

"**Rodney** is a good listener and easy to read to. I took THESE photos for Miss Jam's NEW **Read with Rodney** display wall too."

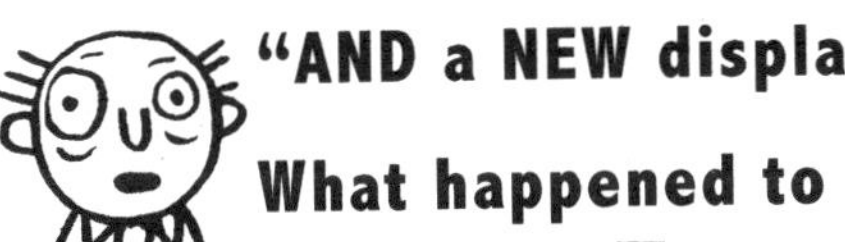

"AND a NEW display wall ... already. What happened to my OLD display wall?" Mr Fullerman wonders.

"Miss Jam took it all down. She's put up LOADS more pictures around the whole classroom!" I tell him.

I'm KEEN to share the FRIDAY **PIE DAY** news too.

"AND that's not all, sir – Miss Jam has set up FRIDAY **PIE DAY** where we get to taste different pies from different places. We're all VERY EXCITED!"

"I can tell," Mr Fullerman mutters as more kids from my class start arriving.

"It's GREAT, sir! Can we keep **Read with Rodney Rat** when you come back, sir?"

Mark Clump wants to know.

"And keep being a daily helper for EXTRA stars!"

Marcus joins in.

"Please can we keep FRIDAY **PIE DAY?"**

I ask Mr Fullerman.

"I LOVE FRIDAY **PIE DAY!"**

Brad shouts randomly.

"I'm not sure. We'll have to see..."

Mr Fullerman tells us.

"HOORAY! Mr Fullerman said YES!" Brad shouts.

"Hang on, Brad – that's not what I said..."

Straight away, everyone starts chanting:

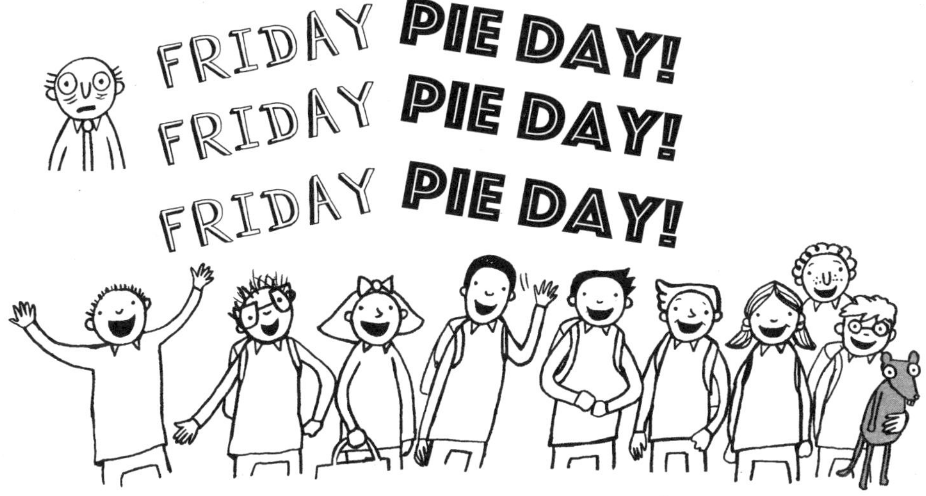

We keep the chant going all the way to our classrooms.

Miss Jam is waiting to high-five us all as we walk in.

"Did I hear you all say 'FRIDAY **PIE DAY**'?" she asks with a big smile on her face.

"We were telling Mr Fullerman what a BRILLIANT idea it is, Miss Jam," I tell her.

Miss Jam is just as enthusiastic today as she was yesterday.

(Maybe even a bit more.)

"Good MORNING, Class 5J - is everyone ready for a quick-fire SUPER spelling session? It's going to be SO much FUN."

(Oh.)

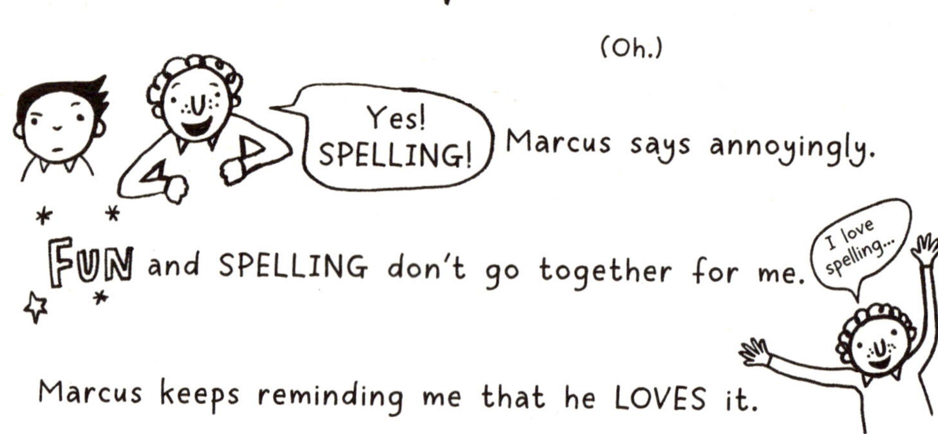

Marcus says annoyingly.

FUN and SPELLING don't go together for me.

Marcus keeps reminding me that he LOVES it.

It's even annoying AMY and she loves spelling too.

While Miss Jam gets the test ready, Mark Clump hands **Rodney Rat** and the tiny suitcase back to Miss Jam.

"Did you enjoy reading to **Rodney?**"
Miss Jam asks him.

"I did! I read a book about SPIDERS while my brother took some photos for the display."

"OH! Mark – these are ... great. I can SEE that YOU really enjoyed reading to **Rodney,**" Miss Jam says.

She adds the pictures to the display and it's true – Mark DOES look like he's having the **BEST** time...

Rodney Rat ... not so much.

READ WITH Rodney Rat Where has Rodney BEEN?

Mark Clump had spiders and a snake to READ with Rodney Rat.

Rodney looks more relaxed on

Miss Jam's desk.

(For now.)

"Miss Jam!"

AMY calls out.

"Whose turn is it to READ WITH **Rodney** next?"

(Good point, Amy.)

We ALL put up our hands and say:

"Pleeeeeeaaaassssseeeeeee, missssssss!"

(Miss Jam is not swayed by our BEGGING.)

"I've made a list so you'll all get a turn – if you want one," she says, and pins the list up near the photo display.

Unless there's a new, second Tom in the class – then it's ME! I'm NEXT on the list to Read with **Rodney**. YES!

"Miss Jam, I'm READY to Read with **Rodney**!"

AMY high-fives me – Marcus just pulls a face.

"Miss Jam, how long are you going to be our teacher for? Because we all want the chance to Read with **Rodney**," **AMY** asks.

(Good question, Amy.)

"Mr Keen will need a bit of time to recover from his **SPORTS injury**. So you're STUCK with me as your teacher for now!"

Everyone startes to cheer...

Hooray for Miss Jam!

Hooray for Miss Jam being our TEACHER! Miss Jam is ...

... the BEST teacher EVER!

We're still cheering when Mr Fullerman walks into the classroom.

"Hello, Class 5F – I heard cheering and wondered what the good news is..."

"Hello, Mr Fullerman, can I help you?" Miss Jam asks.

"I'm just admiring the NEW display.

But I can see you're busy – and I'm busy too – so I'll leave you to it,"

he says, not moving at all.

Florence puts up her hand and asks,

"Mr Fullerman, what sport WAS Mr Keen doing when he was injured?"

"Mr Keen didn't say. But I'm sure he'll be back at school as soon as possible."

Mr Fullerman smiles at Miss Jam.

Miss Jam smiles back – still waiting for Mr Fullerman to leave.

(But he doesn't move.)

"Right, Class 5F, I've got lots of important work to do, so I'd best be off..."

Mr Fullerman spots that the sign on our door has been changed to:

Miss Jam – 5J

"Everyone say GOODBYE to Mr Fullerman. I need to choose my HELPER for today – AND we have our SUPER-DUPER spelling test to look forward to!

Who's excited about that?"

Miss Jam asks.

I'm not – but I still CHEER along with the rest of the class as Miss Jam closes the door behind Mr Fullerman.

I try my best in the spelling test, but some words I ALWAYS spell rong – rung – or wrong?

(Silent w's are tricky – who invented them?)

"Hey, Tom, did you make another **comic?**" **AMY** asks me.

"Yes, it's in my bag," I say happily.

Marcus suddenly perks up.

"I'm making my own comic," he tells us.

"What's your **comic** about?" I ask him with a sigh.

"I can't tell you, but it's SO good," he says proudly.

"Can we see it?" **AMY** asks.

"No – it's not ready yet," says Marcus.

"You can see my **comic** if you want to, **AMY**. But don't let anyone else read it."

I take it out of my bag quietly and slide it over to her.

Marcus is all EYES.

"Have you drawn Mr Keen as an ant?" he asks, peering at it.

"I might have..." I whisper.

"Is he on a **unicycle**? You'll get into BIG trouble if he sees this."

"Shhhh, they're just ants in pants and Mr Keen will NEVER see it."

AMY reads my **comic** and she's trying not to LAUGH, but her shoulders are SHAKING.

Miss Jam looks over and smiles – in a way that means to be quiet.

BE QUIET

"Write your name at the top of the paper and NO talking, please."

She stares in our direction.

"The first word to spell is BICYCLE."

AMY tries not to LAUGH.

"Is something FUNNY in the front row?"

Miss Jam wants to know.

AMY shakes her head and writes BICYCLE down with a smiley face. I'm looking at AMY's work (not copying, just making sure mine is the same as hers) when my **comic** falls off AMY's lap and slides on to the floor right BEHIND me.

Oh!

Leroy sees it, then reaches out his FOOT and drags it towards himself.

Which is GOOD.

Ha!
Ha!
Ha!

Then he picks it up and starts reading it.

NO!

He starts LAUGHING as well.

Miss Jam looks up.

Leroy quickly passes my **comic** to Indrani and SHE reads it and starts LAUGHING.

Ha!
Ha!
Ha!

Then she gives it to Trevor, who reads it, then passes it to Amber, who GIGGLES.

Miss Jam keeps looking over – she knows something is going round the class.

Ha! Ha! Ha!

It's an odd feeling...

I'm proud my **comic** is making kids LAUGH, but I'm nervous that Miss Jam will SEE IT.

Florence points out.

(More laughing.)

Miss Jam stands up and begins to WALK to the back of the classroom. Mark Clump passes the **comic** to ...

Brad Galloway, who reads it and then

gives it to ...

... Miss Jam.

"Thank you, BRAD -

I'll take that."

(Oh NO!)

"IS this YOUR **comic?**"

she asks him.

'NO, Miss Jam."

"Whose **COMIC** is it?"

Everyone knows it's mine, but no one says a word.

"So this doesn't belong to ANYone?"

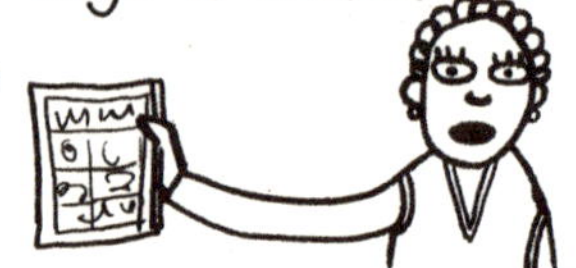

(I keep quiet.)

"Well, if it doesn't belong to anyone, then I'll put it IN THE BIN!"

"NO, Miss Jam! It's MINE!" I say.

Marcus is pointing at me as well.

"Did YOU draw this **comic** in class, Tom?"

"That depends," I say.

"On what, Tom?"

"On if I'm in trouble," I say quietly.

"You're not – but don't draw **comics** during lesson time. You can have it back at the end of the day," she tells me, then puts my **comic** into her drawer and slams it SHUT.

"Sorry, Tom – it just fell off my lap. It's a very good **comic**," **AMY** whispers.

"Glad you liked it."

"It's **FUNNY**," she adds.

"I'm glad Miss Jam didn't READ it and doesn't know WHO it's about," I whisper.

"Unlike the WHOLE class," **AMY** reminds me.

"I just need to get it back now," I sigh.

"Good luck with that." Marcus decides to join in. He's still pointing at me.

At break time, Derek comes to find me, **CHALK** in hand.

"You said you wanted to do more drawing, Tom – remember?"

"My drawings keep getting me into trouble. Miss Jam took my comic away," I tell Derek.

"You'll get it back. We just need to find a good place for one of your impressive **chalk doodles.** Everyone will LOVE it, even Miss Jam," Derek says.

"OK, I'll do it."

We start looking around, but we can't find a space anywhere.

"Tina's been busy," Derek says.

She's already got a BIG CROWD of kids watching her draw round a window frame.

"I've got an idea – follow me," Derek whispers, and takes me to the entrance of the school.

"This is PERFECT. Everyone will walk past here and see YOUR drawing, Tom.
Now what are you going to draw?" Derek asks me.

(Good question.)

"Something that Miss Jam will like and will get me back in her good books!" I say.

Then I wait for INSPIRATION,

but my mind's gone ...

BLANK.

"I can't think of anything to doodle," I say.

"You're kidding? Come on, Tom. If Tina - who's only a little kid - can do it, SO can YOU.

We're running out of time!"

Derek tells me (which isn't helping).

I'm feeling the PRESSURE of the BIG empty space. It HAS to be a good doodle. Derek is waiting for me to start.

"OK, OK, I'll do my best."

Here I go.

I do my signature stars and patterns, and draw as fast as I can until...

Ta-DA! I've drawn **Rodney Rat** (and a small bug).

I stand back and admire my work.

"That's AMAZING, Tom!" Derek's impressed.

"Thanks. We should show it to Miss Jam. She's on break-time duty. Let's go and find her!"

Miss Jam is standing in front of Tina's drawing, along with a bunch of kids, admiring it.

"Miss Jam, would you like to come and see MY drawing?" I say.

"There's a lot of nice artwork being made in this school. I know you're keen on drawing, Tom – let's see what you've been up to." She smiles.

"It's over here, Miss Jam," Derek says.

"I think you're going to LOVE it," I say confidently.

Teachers have stinky socks
Get LOST
OAKFIELD SCHOOL is RUBBISH and so are all the teachers
I HATE School
Read with Rodney

"YOU did THIS, Tom?"

Miss Jam is shocked.

SOMEONE has added EXTRA-BAD doodles and rude writing ALL over **Rodney Rat!**

"YES - no - it wasn't ME or Derek!"

I try and explain.

"Tom did the drawing but not the writing. I just did a few stars," says Derek, trying to back me up.

"I only did the nice drawing, not the stinky socks, the scar, pants, drool or the hair."

Miss Jam doesn't look convinced.

Back in class, Mrs Mumble makes an announcement over the tannoy.

"Caretaker Stan has asked that no one draws anything in chalk on the walls from now on. Chalk drawings are BANNED. Finished, no more, done. Thank you!"

Everyone in class is looking at ME like it's all my fault.

I'll never get my **comic** back at this rate.

Home time can't come soon enough.

The clock seems to be going extra slowly all afternoon.

After everything that's happened, I'm hoping Miss Jam is STILL going to let me READ with **Rodney Rat**, as it IS my turn.

"Everyone, it's nearly home time and, Tom..."

"Yes, Miss Jam?"

"Look after **Rodney Rat**. I'm trusting you to take very good care of him. Read him a story and bring in the pictures for the display tomorrow. He's a very special rat to me."

"I WILL, Miss Jam, I promise! I know exactly where I'm going to read with him!" I say.

This is helping me forget about the wall doodle and who did it. Instead I take **Rodney Rat** and enjoy tapping Marcus on the head and pretending **Rodney** can talk.

"Hello, Marcus," I say in a squeaky rat voice.

"Stop that, Tom."

"It's not Tom – it's Rodney!"

I squeak some more.

Then I stand in front of the class and **WAVE** goodbye.

"See you tomorrow," I squeak.

Hilarious, Tom. Marcus says.

"I am..." I squeak back.

Brad Galloway shouts from the back of the classroom...

"WE LOVE YOU, **Rodney Rat**!"

Which is unexpected.

"He's SO cute!" Amber Tulley Green says.

The RAT, not you, Tom... says Marcus.

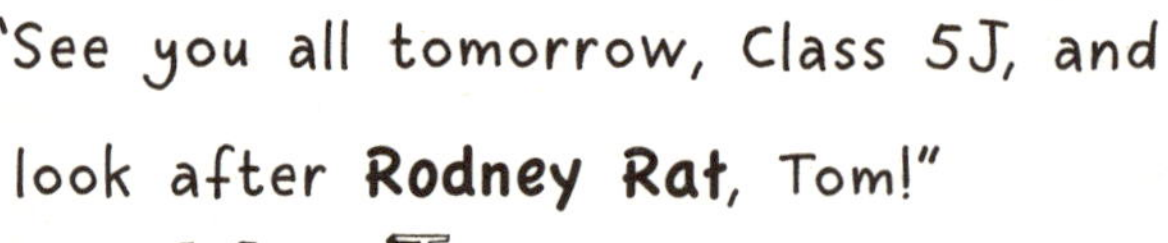

"See you all tomorrow, Class 5J, and look after **Rodney Rat**, Tom!"

Miss Jam tells me as I leave.

Derek's waiting for me where my drawing had been. Thanks to Caretaker Stan, it's all gone, but that doesn't stop some kids walking past and talking about me.

He's the one who wrote the rude stuff!

Thanks to Tom, no one can draw on the walls any more.

"Hey, it **wasn't** ME!" I try to explain.

"Take no notice, Tom. I know it wasn't you ... even if the WHOLE school thinks it was," Derek tells me.

"Someone else must have done it when we went to get Miss Jam," I say.

"SOMEONE who can draw quickly," Derek adds.

"Like that little kid Tina – she could have done it!" I suggest.

"Really? But now SHE can't draw on the wall any more either."

"True..." I put on my squeaky rat voice and say,

"If you ask me, she's suspicious."

Derek pretends to shake **Rodney**'s paw.

"Can I come round tonight and READ while we do band practice?" **Rodney** squeaks.

"Sure, but only if you stop using that annoying voice," Derek tells me.

I squeak in a lower tone to make it different.

"OK."

"That's still annoying, Tom."

As we're leaving the school grounds, I spot Mr Fullerman in Mr Keen's office.

He's still working, I think.

I **LIFT** **Rodney** up as high as I can to get his attention, then **SHOUT**:

"BYEEEEE, Mr Fulllerman! FROM Rodney Rat!"

He doesn't hear me.

"Do me a favour, Tom?" Derek asks.

"Sure!"

"No more **Rodney Rat** voice – it's painful."

"I'll do my best."

The **GOOD NEWS** is I get to introduce **Rodney Rat** to Delia, who's sitting in the kitchen quietly reading. (But not for long.)

"AGH! Don't do that, Tom!" she shouts as I make **Rodney** ruffle her hair.

"It's not ME, it's Rodney Rat. He's come to say, 'Hello, Delia!'"

I squeak in my high-pitched **Rodney Rat** voice.

"Hilarious, Tom - take **Rodney** AWAY."

"He likes you though - he likes reading too.

We're just getting snacks to take to Derek's.

Don't make **Rodney** SAD!"

"I'm sad..." I squeak.

"Mum's bought more chocolate spread so you won't eat mine. Now leave me alone." Delia pushes **Rodney** away.

"It wasn't **ME** who left the empty chocolate spread in the garden. I know who **REALLY** did it. Derek told me it was Mum!"

"Nice try, Tom. Now, off you go," Delia tells me.

"But it's TRUE!" I say in my real voice.

"What's true?" Dad asks, popping his head round the door.

"Nothing – Tom's making up stories again," Delia says, which makes me **cross.**

"It's not a story, it's true. Derek told me!"

"It must be true then, if Derek said so!" Delia says.

Dad points to **Rodney**.

"Who's that then, Tom?"

"It's **Rodney** – the rat I told you about. I've brought him home for extra reading and photos for Miss Jam's display."

"Ah! **Rodney**'s a TOY rat. Very funny, Tom!" Dad says.

"It's not THAT FUNNY..." Delia adds.

"And what are you going to READ with **Rodney?**" Dad wants to know.

"That BOOK **The History of Guitars** on the high shelf."

"GOOD CHOICE, Tom! I'll get it down for you," Dad says. "But don't stay too late at the Fingles'. You spend <u>more</u> time there than in your own house sometimes!"

"We won't," I say in my squeaky rat voice.

"RIGHT! Back to my shed for some more..."

I ask hopefully.

No, Tom... Work.
And no chocolate spread.

Dad smiles.

"That wasn't me - it was Mum!"

I say, but Dad's gone.

"BYE, Tom. Stay as late as you want at the Fingles'." Delia waves.

"It <u>WAS</u> Mum who finished the chocolate spread,' I say again.

But Delia has put on her headphones.

I'm going to tell Derek.

<u>HE</u> listens to me...

"SO, I told Delia it was MUM who ate the chocolate spread and SHE said–"

"This book is **brilliant**, Tom – can I borrow it after you've read it?"

"No, that's not what she said ... and YES you can borrow it, Derek," I sigh.

Rooster keeps sniffing **Rodney Rat**, which is distracting me.

"Leave **Rodney** alone!" Derek tells him, which doesn't work as Rooster's not listening either.

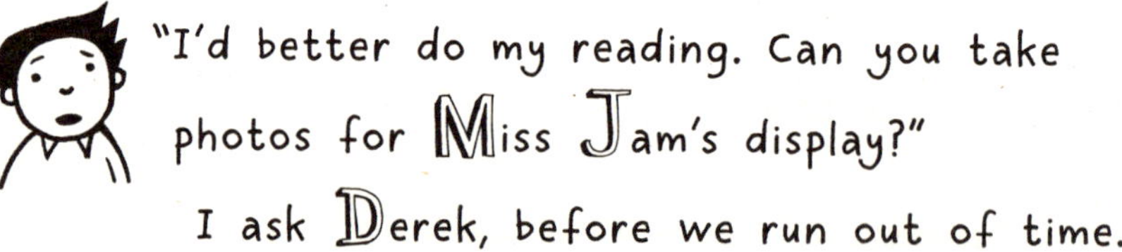

"I'd better do my reading. Can you take photos for Miss Jam's display?" I ask Derek, before we run out of time.

"Sorry, Tom, did you say something?"

"I'll do it..." I tell Derek, and let him read for a bit longer. It's fun setting up the photos and Derek takes good pictures.

(In the end.)

Then we sit and read about GUITARS for a bit longer, until I have to go home.

"Where's **Rodney Rat** gone?" I ask Derek, as I can't see him ANYWHERE.

"Rooster might have taken him," says Derek.

Derek calls out, and then we both *RUN* around his house looking for them both.

"Everything all right, boys?" Derek's dad, Mr Fingle, asks.

"Which way did Rooster go?" Derek asks.

"He's in the front garden playing with a NEW TOY!" Mr Fingle says. We run to the window just in time to see...

Mr Akedo's car driving away with **Rodney Rat** on the ROOF.

THIS IS A DISASTER!

"WE HAVE TO STOP MR AKEDO BEFORE IT'S TOO LATE!" I shout.

"IT'S TOO LATE!" Derek shouts back.

"Was that your toy rat, Tom?" Mr Fingle asks me.

"No, it was Miss Jam's. I HAVE to get it BACK!"

"I'm sure someone will tell Mr Akedo he's got a purple stuffed toy rat on the roof of his car, Tom," says Mr Fingle, trying to reassure me.

"IF Mr Akedo BRAKES suddenly, **Rodney** will FLY OFF the roof and I'll never find him!" I say dramatically.

"I could send Rooster out to sniff him out – as it's kind of his fault?" Derek suggests.

"Rooster might make things WORSE – you can't trust him!" I say.

Rooster whimpers like he knows he's done something wrong.

"Do your mum or dad have Mr Akedo's number? They could try calling him and say Rodney's on the car roof?" Mr Fingle suggests.

"That's a good idea. I'll go home and ask," I say, then *HOTFOOT* it back before **Rodney Rat** is LOST forever!

When I tell Mum and Dad what happened, they are very sympathetic and want to help.

Oh no!

Delia is not so helpful.

That's HILARIOUS, Tom. I wish I'd seen it.

"It's not funny, Delia – I have to take **Rodney Rat** back to Miss Jam TOMORROW. I've got to find him."

"You will, Tom. We don't have Mr Akedo's number, but we could always try and buy another **Rodney Rat** – just in case," Mum says.

"There's only ONE **Rodney Rat** and Miss Jam will notice. I don't want to get into any MORE trouble!" I blurt out.

"What do you mean MORE trouble?" Mum asks.

"Nothing! Losing **Rodney** wasn't MY fault," I add quickly.

"Errr, it kind of WAS your fault, Tom. You never take the blame for anything."

"Can we go and CHECK outside and see if **Rodney**'s fallen OFF anywhere?" I ask, not wanting to waste any more time.

"I'll do that, Tom. I'll have a quick drive around the streets – he might have fallen off," Dad says.

"Can I come with you?"

"It's getting late, Tom. I'm SURE we'll find **Rodney Rat** soon – don't worry," Mum tells me.

"Or not. You know Mr Akedo's gone on holiday?"

Delia says.

"HOW DO YOU KNOW HE'S GONE ON HOLIDAY?"

"He was putting a suitcase in the boot of his car – so he's going somewhere,"

Delia adds.

Oh no...

Rodney Rat could be ANYWHERE.

I can't sleep...

I keep thinking about where **Rodney Rat** could be and what Miss Jam is going to say. I'll never get my **comic** back now.

I hope Dad finds him.

Or that Mr Akedo realizes **Rodney** is on his roof and keeps him safe until he is back from his holiday.

Fingers crossed.

Real rat

In the morning, Derek holds up a sign in his window asking about **Rodney**.

I reply...

Mum and Dad didn't find him last night either, but they'll keep looking... We all will.

Mum gives me a note for Miss Jam that EXPLAINS everything. ☺

"You said she's a nice teacher, Tom. I'm SURE she'll understand."

"She might not – I'd be annoyed," Delia says, deciding to join in. ☹

"At least Derek's dad sent me all the photos we took last night. I can still put them up on the display," I say, being positive.

That's something.

"Don't forget your lunch box, Tom," Mum reminds me.

"It's delicious..." Delia says. 

She'd better **NOT** have helped herself. I give her a LOOK before going to meet Derek.

We walk to school quietly, still searching for any sign of **Rodney Rat**...

(Nothing so far.)

"Just think, Tom, you'll be able to put ALL this stuff into a **comic** - like you did with Mr Keen - and LAUGH about it. Miss Jam might even think it's FUNNY,"

Derek tells me, but I'm not so sure.

Or she'll confiscate it, like the last one I drew. Miss Jam put it in a drawer.

How are you going to get it back?

Derek wants to know.

Find **Rodney Rat**, for a start.

It's bad enough that Miss Jam thinks I'm the one who DREW the bad stuff on the wall, THEN she took my **comic** away. Now **Rodney Rat**'s missing AND my classmates think I'm spoiling their drawing fun.

Have you got a PLAN B – just in case?

I've got a NOTE from Mum.

A real one?

YES – I'm not **Buster Jones!**

I say, as that's exactly the sort of thing he'd do.

Mr Fullerman is at the school gates ... along with Marcus, AMY and Florence.

Marcus has his notebook with him and is already writing things down.

"Good morning, everyone," Mr Fullerman says slowly (like he's a bit tired).

"Morning, Mr Fullerman," Derek and I say together.

"Tom took **Rodney Rat** home to read with last night, didn't you, Tom?" AMY tells Mr Fullerman.

"Good for you, Tom. I hope you had fun."

(I keep quiet.)

"I can't WAIT until it's MY TURN to read with **Rodney Rat**!" Florence says to Mr Fullerman.

(Gulp.)

"Did you take some good photos for the display?"

AMY asks.

"Derek did..."

"Let's see them," Marus says.

"Not now - they're in my bag..." I reply.

"I'm glad Miss Jam and Rodney Rat are <u>so</u> popular," Mr Fullerman tells us.

"And FRIDAY **PIE DAY,** sir - don't forget that," Marcus reminds him.

"How could I? Have a good day, all of you."

"We will, sir!" Marcus says cheerily.

(I won't.)

"Good luck, Tom," Derek says as we go into class.

"What do you need good luck for?" Marcus wants to know.

"Nothing," I say. (This is not true.)

He keeps asking where **Rodney** is.

"Is he squashed up in your bag?"

"Don't worry about it, Marcus."

Miss Jam is waiting for us outside our class and looks very HAPPY.

"Morning, all! Tom, did you you read with **Rodney Rat** and have lots of FUN?" She wants to know.

Sort of... I've got pictures... And a very important note.

"Excellent, we'll add them to the display. Just put **Rodney** back on the table."

(This is getting tricky.)

"I'm excited to read with **Rodney Rat** tonight," AMY tells me.

"Don't get too excited..." I warn her.

"Weren't you supposed to put **Rodney** on the table, Tom?" Marcus asks.

"Yup..."

I watch Miss Jam stick up both my photos next to Mark Clump's pictures.

"These are really fabulous pictures, Tom. It makes me SO happy that you're enjoying reading with **Rodney Rat** as much as I did when I was a child. **Rodney** was always my favourite toy," she tells us.

WHAT? OH NO!

(Things just got A LOT worse.)

"WHO'S EXCITED TO READ WITH **Rodney Rat** NEXT?"

The whole class CHEERS and AMY puts up her hand.

"Of course you're next, AMY. Excellent! Tom, would you like to put **Rodney Rat** back on the display table?"

Miss Jam asks me.

"Miss Jam, I have something to say. There's been a tiny problem and my mum's written it all in ... the NOTE ⇨ ✉," I tell her. Miss Jam reads it and her EYES get bigger and BIGGER.

"Class 5J, there's been a change of plan with **Rodney Rat**."

Now the whole class are looking at ME and wondering WHAT I've done! Including AMY.

Brad Galloway shouts from the back of the classroom, "Where's **Rodney Rat**, Miss Jam?"

"He'll be back VERY SOON and cleaner than ever. Thank goodness for that. Isn't that right, Tom?"

'Errrr, yes, Miss Jam..." I say, SURPRISED.

Mum's note seems to have smoothed things over BIG time. MAYBE Mum HAS found **Rodney Rat** after all?

THIS IS GREAT NEWS!

I need to FOCUS on my maths worksheet now, but it's not easy.

AMY keeps asking me questions that are hard to answer.

"Why does **Rodney** need cleaning? What were you doing with him?"

"If I tell you, you have to promise not to say anything," I whisper.

"OK."

I take a deep breath ...

and I'm about to tell AMY about Rooster leaving **Rodney Rat** on top of Mr Akedo's car when Miss Jam interrupts.

"TOM, no talking in class. PLEASE finish this MATHS worksheet. It's very important. We need ALL our work done before FRIDAY **PIE DAY** – IS that clear?"

Miss Jam is being really

Marcus TUTS and shows me his notebook.

He's drawn a sad ☹ face in it and points to me.

I can't reply, as Miss Jam is hovering around and doesn't want any more talking.

So instead I do a drawing...

It takes me a while, but I try to draw EXACTLY what happened to **Rodney Rat**.

Marcus is being NOSY and leaning over to see what I'm doing.

"You heard what Miss Jam said. You should stop drawing and finish your worksheet..."

"I'll do it in a minute."

I slide my drawing over to AMY so she can see what happened.

"Not now, Tom. Miss Jam's watching," she whispers.

Miss Jam suddenly says...

"TOM, is that a completed worksheet for me? I'll be collecting them ALL now."

I HIDE my drawing under my VERY empty worksheet.

Marcus nudges me to say, "Told you..."

Miss Jam, what happens if I haven't finished it and I need a bit more time?

I ask her.

Miss Jam sighs loudly.

(This happens.)

I have to stay after class and finish my worksheet.

I don't want to spoil FRIDAY **PIE DAY** for everyone, so I'm GLAD to do it. (Sort of.)

"How are you doing, Tom?" Miss Jam wants to know.

"Finished!" I say, and do lots of smiling as if NOTHING happened to **Rodney Rat** at all.

"Were you drawing in class again instead of getting on with your work?" she asks me, which is AWKWARD.

"I was just thinking about **Rodney Rat**, Miss Jam, and the TIME *disappeared.*"

(**Rodney Rat** disappeared too but I don't say that.)

"I look forward to YOU bringing **Rodney** back tomorrow and do thank your mum for the note."

"Tomorrow?"

"That's right, Tom, tomorrow. The note was very clear," **M**iss **J**am tells me.

"Tomorrow?" I check again.

"YES. We can do a swap. You'll get your **comic** back at the same time."

"Oh no, that's ... bad," I say quietly, as I wanted my **comic** back today.

"All your classmates seemed to be enjoying your **comic**. I might read it myself," she adds.

"NO! Don't bother, **M**iss **J**am."

I'm trying to put her OFF.

"I do have lots of worksheets to mark, including yours. OFF you go, Tom," she says, and adds my worksheet to the pile.

"Yes, **M**iss **J**am." I smile and casually grab my bag and **Rodney Rat** drawing, which I don't want **M**iss **J**am to see either.

Me being casual

I go and find my friends, who are trying to play **CHAMP** with the little kids.

I say "play" - they're standing around as the little kids are so good they're not getting much of a look-in.

Turns out Tina is good at drawing and amazing at **CHAMP** too.

She's been in the **CHAMP** square the whole time and doesn't look like she's going anywhere soon.

Tina being amazing

AMY, Derek, Florence and Norman are still waiting to have a turn, while Marcus has his notebook out and is writing - who knows what - in it.

"Hey, Tom, if you keep drawing in class, we'll miss out on FRIDAY **PIE DAY!"** he says, like he's telling me off.

"It's all **FINE**. I finished my drawing and she didn't catch me," I reply.

"What did you draw, Tom? Can I see it?" Norman asks me.

"SURE! I'll show you..."

I look inside my bag to find it.

"It's here somewhere," I say.

"What DID happen to **Rodney Rat**, Tom?" Leroy wants to know.

"It's all in my drawing... Hang on."

Everyone is waiting for me to show them my picture.

"Have you forgotten that as well? Maybe it's on your desk," AMY says.

"I hope not!" I say, shaking my bag out on to the ground.

"Is that the **comic** about Mr Keen falling off his **unicycle?** It's SO FUNNY." Florence LAUGHS.

"Thanks - BUT no one is supposed to know it's really about Mr Keen, remember? It's just ANTS IN PANTS."

"I might have told a few people..." Norman says.

"Did you? Like who?" I ask.

"Just all those little kids over there..." He points to Tina and her friends, who are STILL playing **CHAMP**.

"And maybe Class 1B,

Class 2A,

all of Class 5S..."

"Anyone else?"

I say, as this sounds like A **LOT** of kids.

"Errrr, Class 4K, 2B and everyone else I bumped into."

"So, the WHOLE school knows I drew a **comic** about Mr Keen?" I ask Norman.

"NO! Not the whole school. I didn't tell Caretaker Stan."

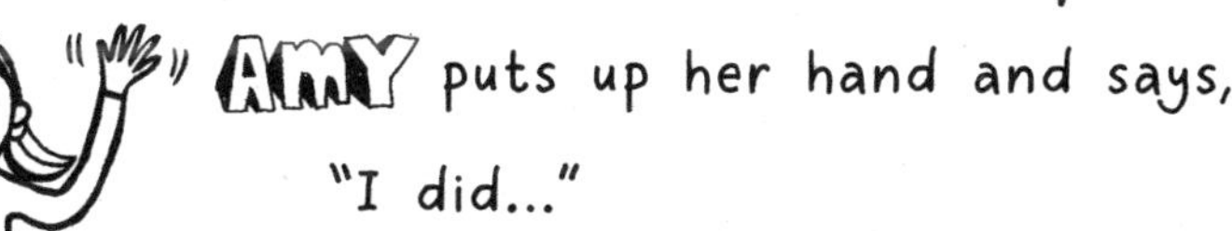

AMY puts up her hand and says, "I did..."

"I bet if Mr Keen saw your **comic**, he'd think it was FUNNY as well," Derek tells me.

"Do you really think so?" I ask.

"No."

"Good news is: Miss Jam said I'd get my **comic** back when I bring **Rodney Rat** into school tomorrow."

DEREK gets EXCITED!

"Does that mean you've FOUND **Rodney Rat?** Why didn't you tell me, Tom?"

He high-fives me.

"My mum must have found him – Miss Jam read Mum's note and said it was all OK," I explain.

"That's BRILLIANT! Rooster will be SO pleased. He's been miserable! Rooster knows he shouldn't have TAKEN **Rodney Rat**, then THROWN him around and played with him in the garden. It was an accident that he CHUCKED **Rodney** on top of Mr Akedo's car. How was he supposed to know that Mr Akedo would DRIVE off with **Rodney** on the roof?"

Tina and the little kids have stopped playing **CHAMP** just to listen to Derek's story.

"Derek's just told you what my drawing was about," I tell everyone.

"Wow... Does Miss Jam know her beloved **Rodney Rat**, her childhood toy, was on Mr Akedo's car roof?" Marcus asks.

No! No!

"She doesn't NEED to know either – not now **Rodney's** safely back and you'll all get your turn to read with him. **Rodney Rat**'s little adventure is our secret."

I smile at my friends.

Then Norman says,

"Don't worry, Tom. Your secret's safe with me!"

Which doesn't make me feel that confident.

I go back to class and SPOT something on Miss Jam's desk.

There's a pile of our maths worksheets and poking out from under my worksheet is what looks like ...

THE DRAWING I DID.

The one I've been LOOKING for.

The drawing that explains EXACTLY what happened to **Rodney Rat**!

The drawing that Miss Jam doesn't need to

SEE.

It's so close I could *LEAN*

over and TAKE it back.

(Good plan.)

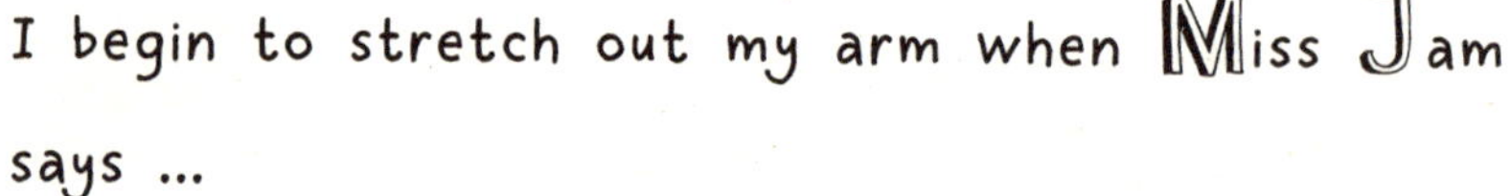

I begin to stretch out my arm when Miss Jam says ...

"Sit down, Tom."

And puts her hand ON top of the worksheets.

There is NO chance of me sneaking it back now.

I keep staring at it ...

... hoping there will be another chance for me to SWIPE my drawing.

Miss Jam is taking the register, but all I can think of is my drawing. So NEAR yet SO FAR.

AMY has to NUDGE me when it's my turn to answer.

"Yes, Miss Jam."

(I'm here ...

but not really.)

I'm trying to think of other ways to get my picture back without Miss Jam noticing.

If I could just get Miss Jam to leave her desk - then I could GRAB it! But HOW?

"Class 5J, I need to pop to the school office to check we can still do PE in the hall. I'll only be gone for two minutes."

(Yes! This is perfect timing.)

"If ANYONE has forgotten their PE kit, you'll need to come with me to the SPARE KIT BOX," Miss Jam adds.

I say.

My face says it all.

I watch Miss Jam pick up the worksheets and my drawing, put them in a box file and close the lid. Any chance of getting my picture back EASILY ... has disappeared.

My drawing!

Oh.

Marcus is pointing at me, so Miss Jam knows ...

... that I don't have my PE kit.

"Hurry up, Tom. I don't want anyone missing out on PE. It's just as well Oakfield School has a **spare kit box**, isn't it?"

I'm not so sure about that...

I get through PE wearing the only thing I could find in the spare kit box. A spotty top and spotty flared tracksuit bottoms.

PE ALMOST takes my mind off the **Rodney Rat** drawing for a bit.

Our lesson is interrupted by an announcement over the tannoy from Mrs Mumble:

"Sorry to disturb lessons, but as it's nearly the end of the day we wanted to SHARE some GOOD NEWS with you all! Mr Keen is coming back to school sooner than we all expected – THIS FRIDAY! Thank you very much and have a great day."

There's a loud cheer in the background that sounds like it could have been Mr Fullerman celebrating.

YES! WOO-HOO!

Today has gone VERY slowly.

The LAST thing Miss Jam said to me as I left to go home was ...

"Tom, don't forget to bring **Rodney Rat** back tomorrow, like your mum promised in her note.

I'll be so happy to see my wonderful childhood toy all clean too."

I say,

and hurry out of the classroom.

I look back to see Miss Jam take the red box file with MY drawing inside and put it in her **BAG.**

Like she's taking it HOME.

(Oh no...)

"You're late..." Derek says when we meet up.

"I know - Miss Jam's got my drawing of **Rodney Rat**. I was trying to get it back and FAILED BIG time."

"But now your mum's found **Rodney**. That's all that matters, right?"

"Oh yeah. I didn't think of that. Miss Jam did say she'd give my **comic** back once **Rodney Rat** was with her again."

"See! There you go, Tom - you're worried about nothing. And Mr Fullerman's going to be your teacher again. He's very HAPPY about that," Derek says.

"How do you know that?
I thought he liked being the
headteacher."

Derek points UP to the office window.

It's true...

He does look very HAPPY.

I'm looking forward to asking Mum where she found **Rodney Rat** and I'm so glad he's safe. When I get home, Mum's waiting for me and says,

"Hi, Tom – I've got a SURPRISE for you!"

"EXCELLENT!" I say.

"Granny and Grandad are here!" Mum adds.

"And they've got a present for you!"

"Is it a **Rodney Rat**-shaped present, Mum?" I ask.

"Hello, Tom. I think you're going to be very happy. Your mum told us what happened. So I got busy..." Granny Mavis says.

"I was no help at all,"
Grandad says honestly.

Then Granny hands me a gift bag with something wrapped up inside.

"THIS is going to make Miss Jam SO HAPPY. It turns out that **Rodney Rat** is her CHILDHOOD toy and she's expecting me to bring him back to school tomorrow, thanks to the note you gave me, Mum.

She wasn't as cross as I think she'd be if she found out that **Rodney** was THROWN on to Mr Akedo's car roof and driven AWAY!" I tell them all.

"So thank you SO much for finding..."

Oh.

It's purple but doesn't look like **Rodney Rat.**

"What happened to **Rodney Rat?**

He looks ... different."

"I tried to knit another **Rodney** from a photo you took of him. There wasn't much time," Granny says.

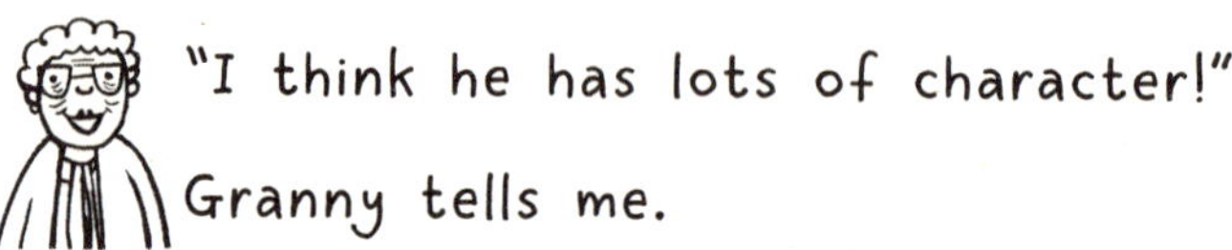

"I think he has lots of character!" Granny tells me.

"It's nice of you to try, Granny. Your note to Miss Jam said that you'd FOUND **Rodney,** Mum!"

"Ermmm. Not exactly, Tom..." Mum says.

"I wanted to give us more time to find him. Dad was still looking! So I wrote that you'd accidentally dropped him in the bath - and we were drying him out," Mum tells me, which means **Rodney Rat** is STILL missing.

"What am I going to give Miss Jam tomorrow then?" I say, as it's a BIG problem.

"You could tell Miss Jam that **RODNEY** has SHRUNK in the wash," Granny suggests.

"Or **Rodney** got HIT by lightning," Grandad adds.

"We'll keep looking, Tom. It's not like she knows **Rodney's** lost ... YET. I don't know why she'd let you take home a toy if it was SO precious to her. Something was bound to happen," Mum says.

Delia arrives home at EXACTLY the wrong moment.

"What's happened to the RAT? He looks like he's been to an all-night party."

"Granny made me a **NEW Rodney Rat** to take to school."

"Respect, Granny! I prefer this version of **Rodney. Rough Rodney!**" Delia LAUGHS.

Then Dad comes back and starts calling out,

"I'm HOME! And GUESS what I've GOT that you're all going to be happy about!"

YES!

Dad has found **Rodney Rat!**

He appears from round the door and IN his hand is ...

... a JAR of chocolate SPREAD!

Awwwwwwwwwwww. I GROAN.

"That's not the reaction I was expecting – I thought you'd all be pleased,"

Dad says, sounding disappointed.

But not as disappointed as ME.

"We thought you'd found **Rodney Rat**, Frank. Tom HAS to return him to Miss Jam tomorrow," Mum tells Dad.

"Who's that then? It looks a bit like **Rodney,"**

Dad wonders.

"That's **Rough Rodney** – he's been out clubbing all night and then dragged through a hedge backwards," Delia says.

"It's not funny, Delia. FRIDAY **PIE DAY** will be cancelled if I don't find the REAL **Rodney** by tomorrow," I tell her.

"It is quite funny, Tom," Delia says, not helping as usual.

"We'll think of SOMETHING, Tom. Don't worry," says Mum.

"Does anyone want some chocolate spread on toast?" Dad offers, hoping to cheer me up.

"I have MY own spread, thanks - that I'm not sharing with anyone," Delia says, glaring at me.

(Through her glasses.)

"I'm OK. I'm not the biggest fan of chocolate spread," Mum announces, which is a BIG SURPRISE. Especially as Derek saw her hiding in the garden and eating chocolate spread straight out of Delia's jar.

I'm about to make THAT point when Granny Mavis tells Dad,

"We won't stay for chocolate spread either. We have to get to our book club!"

"What book did you all read?" he asks her.

"It's a **MYSTERY** adventure called The False Teeth Conspiracy and it's right up my street."

Grandad bites his teeth together quickly. Granny rolls her eyes...

"Any excuse to take out his teeth. Don't do it, Bob! Not everyone shares your sense of humour, especially at the book club," she reminds me.

"What do you mean? I'm hilarious!" Grandad says.

THE FOSSILS head off and I hear **BARKING** coming from outside in the garden. It's Rooster playing with Derek, so I take **Rough Rodney** to show him.

Rough Rodney is kind of growing on me.

Hey, Tom! Have you got **Rodney Rat** back? Let's see him!

Derek calls out.

"Or not..." Derek says, sounding surprised.

"Granny Mavis knitted him. He looks a bit different I know," I say.

"You can say that again..." Derek agrees.

"Mum hadn't really found **Rodney Rat** after all – he's still missing."

I HOLD **Rough Rodney** well away from Rooster, who is jumping up and down very excitedly and SNIFFING **Rodney**.

"Miss Jam's not going to be HAPPY.

She might even cancel FRIDAY **PIE DAY**

and then everyone will blame ME,"

I tell Derek.

"Probably, kids are like that.

I know it wasn't your fault, Tom."

"Thanks, Derek. If ONLY Rooster hadn't taken him though."

"Yeah - Rooster ATE my passport once.

We had to cancel our holiday and Mum was furious.

I wasn't that happy either.

Yes, Rooster, I'm talking about YOU."

Rooster keeps leaping around like nothing is wrong at all.

"Hey, Rooster - do YOU know where **Rodney Rat** is?" I ask him.

Rooster stops, lifts up one ear, then starts barking really loudly.

He's pulling Derek to go inside and won't stop **BARKING.**

"Stop that, Rooster! I think he's hungry, Tom. I'd better go and feed him. He's going nuts," Derek says.

I make **Rough Rodney** wave goodbye. "See you tomorrow."

"And don't forget, Tom – Mr Keen's back on Friday, so Miss Jam's not going to be your teacher for much longer."

"That's true."

Derek is always good at making me feel better.

Though I don't think Miss Jam will EVER give me back my **comic** now.

Mum is also making helpful suggestions.

"I can send an email to the school office, or write you another note, Tom?"

"And this time you could just tell Miss Jam the TRUTH, Rita. That's the best thing to do," Dad says to Mum, who gives him a LOOK.

"I was only trying to buy us a bit more time, Frank. I didn't think a purple toy rat was going to be that hard to find!"

Mum sounds annoyed.

"This note will explain everything properly.

Now off you go to bed and try to get some sleep."

I'll do my best.

I take **Rough Rodney** up to my room and sit him at the bottom of my bed.

He looks comfy there.

Derek is at his window holding up a sign that says he's going to the dentist in the morning. So I draw him a sign with a **smiley** tooth, which he likes.

Then I get ready for bed and try to have a good sleep.

I forget all about **Rough Rodney** until ...

... I wake up on Friday morning.
Rough Rodney is STARING at me.

(Meanwhile Rooster is dreaming.)

I talk to **Rough Rodney** as I get out of bed and head to the bathroom.

Delia's outside, knocking on the door.

"Hurry up, Tom – who are you talking to in there?"

So, obviously, I take my time.

"Did you hear that, **Rodney?** Delia wants us to be quick."

EVENTUALLY I hold **Rough Rodney** out of the door and say,

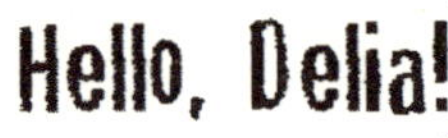

in a DEEP voice.

"So annoying..." (She's not impressed.)

Downstairs, Mum makes sure the note for Miss Jam is IN my bag.

"Don't forget to give this to Miss Jam, and hopefully she'll understand that accidents happen and we haven't given up on finding **Rodney Rat** yet."

"Thanks, Mum, fingers crossed," I agree. Derek is at the dentist this morning, so I'm walking to school on my own.

As I go past the corner shop, I get a STRONG urge for a snack. A quick look in my bag reminds me that I don't have any money.

No money = no snack.

When I get to school, Mr Fullerman is at the gates saying good morning to everyone. Suddenly Mr KEEN APPEARS and says,

"Hello, EVERYONE – I'm back!"

then he starts waving like he's been away for AGES and not just a few days.

Mr Keen looks happy, but not as HAPPY as Mr Fullerman.

He's almost jumping for joy.

Marcus has spotted me and comes running over.

"Tom – did you bring **Rodney Rat** back?"

"Kind of."

"That's GOOD, because Miss Jam wasn't very pleased with you yesterday," he enjoys reminding me.

AMY and Norman join us and ask me the same thing. "Have you got Rodney in your bag, Tom? Can I see him?" says Norman, jumping around.

"Wait until we get into class."

"Who's ready for FRIDAY **PIE DAY** then?" AMY says.

This sets off another CHANT – even kids who don't know what it is join in.

"FRIDAY **PIE DAY** – FRIDAY **PIE DAY!**"

Buster Jones hears the chant and now HE wants to know what FRIDAY **PIE DAY** is all about.

"Hey, Gatesy, what's going on?"

"Our supply teacher, Miss Jam, says we can do a pie tasting on Fridays."

"That sounds MAD. Hey, meet me at lunch time – I have something I want you to do," Buster tells me.

THIS doesn't sound good.

Buster is always getting into trouble OR getting other kids into trouble – sometimes BOTH at the same time.

I RUSH to class and the FIRST thing I see on Miss Jam's desk is ...

... the drawing I did of **Rodney Rat**!

It's THERE, just poking out from under the maths worksheets.

Miss Jam has been marking them and looks up when I come in.

"Good morning, Tom. Do you have something for me?"

Marcus interrupts before I can say a WORD. "Tom's got **Rodney Rat** in his bag, Miss Jam."

"That's excellent news! I was VERY worried you'd lost him, Tom, or something TERRIBLE had happened to my **Rodney Rat**."

I try to act relaxed and laugh. "Ha! Ha! Rodney had a very BORING time with me and didn't DO anything or GO anywhere at all."

Ha! Ha!

(WHY did I say that?)

"Firstly, Class 5J," Miss Jam says, "you'll be PLEASED to hear that Mr Keen is BACK and fully recovered from his SPORTS injury."

Norman starts to giggle, making Miss Jam stop speaking.

"Is something funny, Norman?"

"No, Miss Jam."

"I'll continue. Today – FRIDAY – we can celebrate Mr Keen AND **Rodney Rat**'s return with a special PIE tasting. MY pie is in the staffroom in case you're wondering where it is."

(I have other things on my mind.)

"Tom, please put **Rodney Rat** BACK on the display table."

Now the WHOLE class is waiting to see **Rodney Rat**.

I take him out of my bag and there's a loud GASP...

Miss Jam holds her hand over her mouth in **SHOCK**.

"What on EARTH happened to **Rodney?**"

"He's been squashed up in my bag. He's OK and I have a NOTE!" I say quickly, and search around in my bag to find it – but it's disappeared.

DO have a note, SOMEWHERE!" I say frantically, then turn my bag upside down and let everything fall out.

The note has ... GONE.

Miss Jam picks up **Rough Rodney** for a closer look.

"This is VERY disappointing, Tom. I was expecting **Rodney** to be clean and soft, not lumpy and cross! He doesn't look like MY **Rodney Rat** any more! What HAVE you done to him?" she says sadly.

"I can explain, Miss Jam..."

I'm trying my best to smooth things over, but it's not working.

"He still looks cute, Miss Jam!" AMY tells her.

"The rat - not you, Tom," Marcus says, like I didn't already know.

"I'm **shocked**, Tom - poor **Rodney.**"

Miss Jam shakes her head.

"BUT, Miss Jam, if you could only read my note..." I'm trying to explain when there's a knock at the door.

Knock Knock!

We all look over to see who it is.

It's Mr Fullerman! Brad Galloway shouts like we've forgotten what he looks like.

Mr Fullerman is holding a tray and can't open the door, so Miss Jam does it for him.

He STRIDES in, smiling with what looks like ...

a PIE.

"Morning, Miss Jam and Class 5F! I heard it was Friday Pie Day, so I thought I'd bring in one of MY favourite pies and join in the fun."

"Oh... I'm sorry, Mr Fullerman. I'm afraid FRIDAY **PIE DAY** has just been **CANCELLED,"** says Miss Jam.

"Awwwwwwwwwwwwwwwww," we all say.

"But what happened? You were ALL looking forward to FRIDAY PIE DAY."

"It's not the right time for a PIE celebration,"

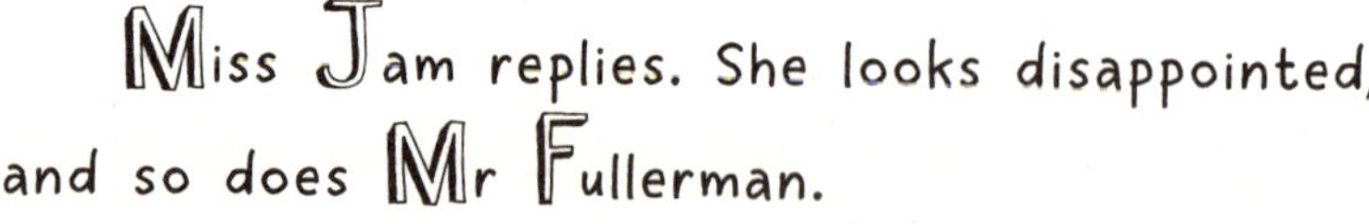

Miss Jam replies. She looks disappointed, and so does Mr Fullerman.

Rough Rodney has slumped over on the display table, like he's given up.

"Is Read with **Rodney Rat** cancelled too?" **AMY** asks.

"Yes, **AMY**. **Rodney** is no longer up to it. Mr Fullerman can do something else when he returns on Monday."

"That's a good idea, Miss Jam. In case you change your mind about Friday Pie Day, I'll take this back to the staffroom and put it right next to the one you made," Mr Fullerman says, trying to make things better.

"I won't change my mind."

"I'll see you on MONDAY, Class 5F."

The atmosphere is TENSE as Mr Fullerman leaves.

"Let's get back to our work," Miss Jam tells us all.

THIS is easier said than done.

Especially for ME.

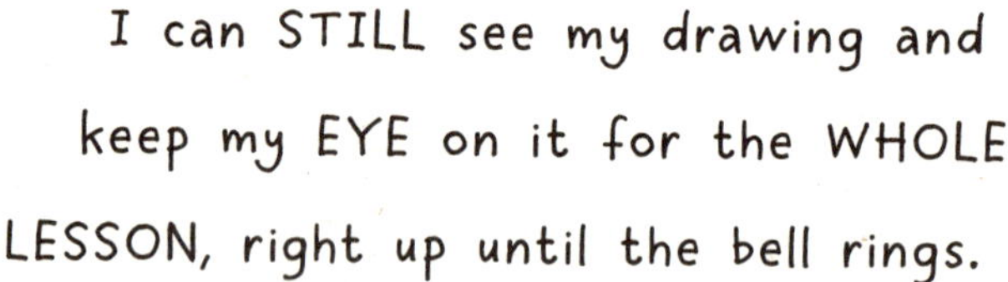

I can STILL see my drawing and keep my EYE on it for the WHOLE LESSON, right up until the bell rings.

Miss Jam pops ALL our worksheets AND my drawing into the box and closes the lid.

"Are you OK, Tom?" AMY asks.

"Not really..." I sigh.

Miss Jam stands up and says,

"**AMY**, could you be my helper and bring a few things downstairs with me?"

"Sorry, Tom. I have to go," **AMY** tells me, and goes off to help Miss Jam.

I head outside for break time and watch Miss Jam carry my **Rodney Rat** drawing with her.

She's BOUND to see it now.

The chances of me EVER getting my ANTS IN PANTS **comic** back are looking like ...

ZERO. ☹

Everything is going wrong.

Meanwhile in the staffroom, the teachers tuck into Mr Fullerman's pie and Miss Jam's pie for FRIDAY **PIE DAY.**

They start a PIE chart as well.

Oakfield School Teachers' favourite PIE.

What's YOUR pie?

PIE CHART

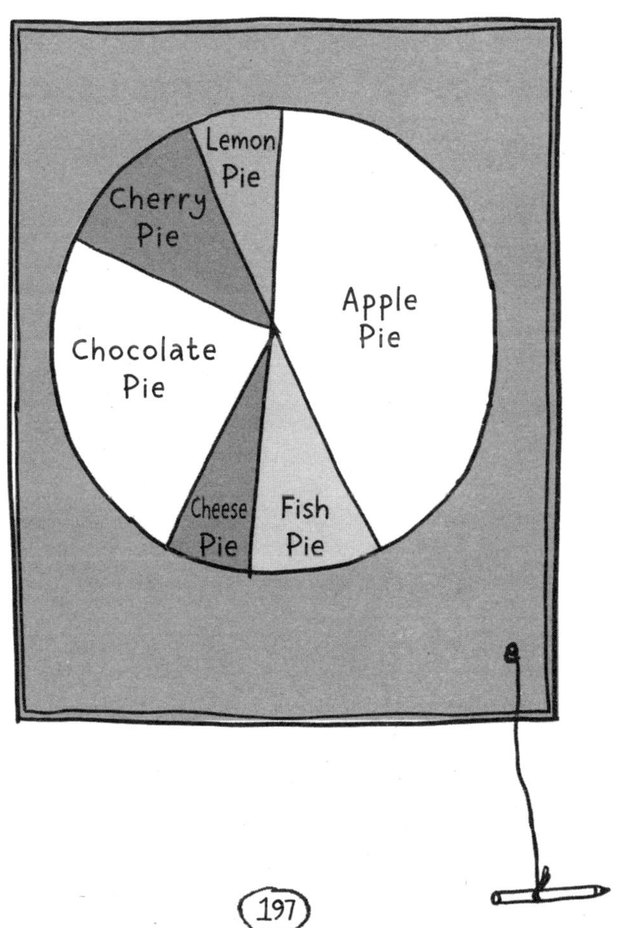

I'd almost forgotten that **Buster Jones** wants to see me.

So the best thing I can do is ... **HIDE.** Sitting behind a LARGE plant pot does the trick.

It's going well, until Norman accidentally kicks a football right into the plant.

I throw it back FAST and Norman SHOUTS...

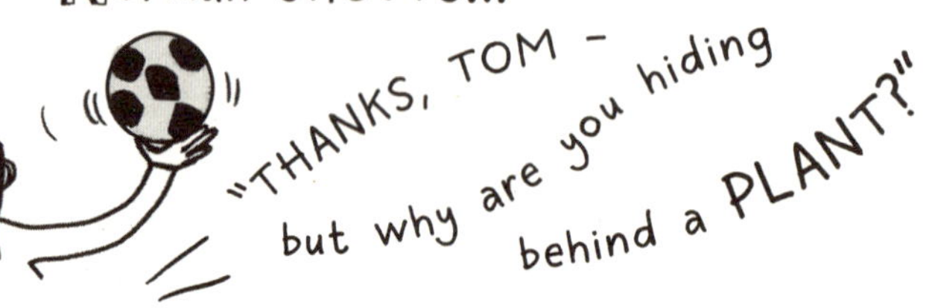

Everyone HEARS him, including **BUSTER JONES.**

"There you are, Gatesy. I've been looking everywhere for you!"

"Have you?"

"Yes, the whole school has been talking about your comic and how funny it is."

"Really?" (This is news to me).

"Yes – the Ants in Pants comic where you drew Mr Keen as an ANT who rides a unicycle and falls off."

(Buster knows a lot about my comic.)

He takes out a load of CHALK from his pocket.

"You and me – we're going to draw some more FUNNY things on the walls, like last time."

"But ... we're not allowed to draw on the walls – remember?" I say, trying to REASON with Buster.

"Who cares? It was HILARIOUS when I added the speech bubbles to your drawing of the RAT. And teachers DO have stinky socks!"

Buster LAUGHS.

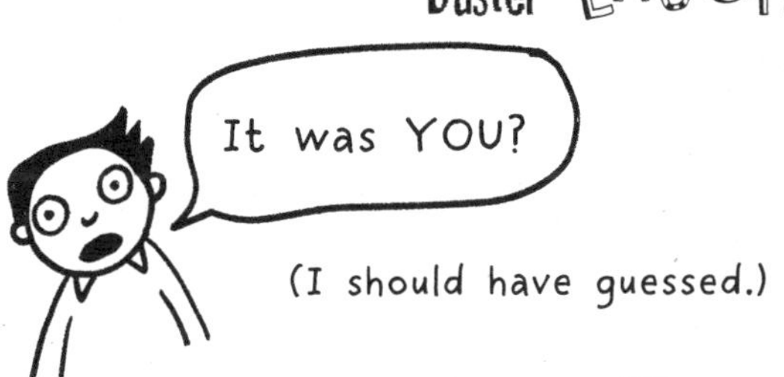

(I should have guessed.)

"Yes – thanks for taking the blame for me, Gatesy."

Buster LAUGHS even more.

"The teachers kept giving me detention and annoying me, so I just expressed myself on your drawing. It was SO funny."

"Not for me it wasn't..." I tell him.

"Fine. YOU don't have to get into trouble because THIS time we can put the blame on that little kid Tina – the one who draws just like you. Everyone will think she did it!"

Buster loves this plan.

"But that's not fair – she's only a little kid, Buster," I remind him.

"OK – YOU can take the blame again – because I'm not."

Buster means business.

"Come on, Gatesy. You draw a picture of Miss Jam as an ant or Mr Fullerman OR Mr Keen falling off a unicycle and I'll write the rude caption."

"No, I don't want to!" I say, sticking up for myself.

"Don't you want your comic back?"

he says, suddenly looking serious.

"Yes, but it's in Miss Jam's drawer," I tell him.

"Not any more," Buster says.

Buster is smiling at me, which is making me nervous.

He lifts his sweatshirt up and THERE'S MY **COMIC!**

"SEE! I've got it, safe and sound."

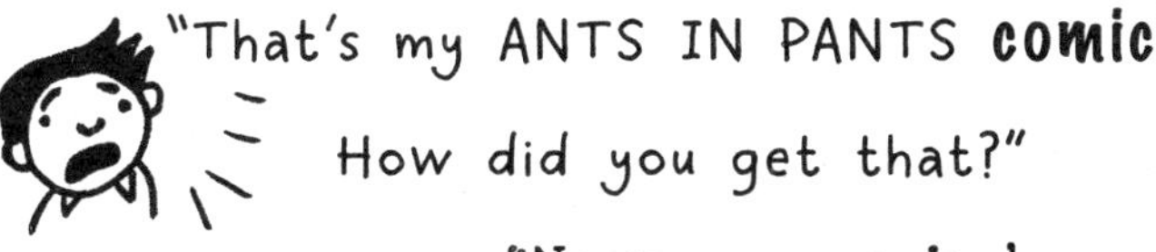

"That's my ANTS IN PANTS **comic!**

How did you get that?"

"Never you mind.

If you want it back, let's get drawing, shall we?"

"Oh..."

I try STALLING for time, walking behind Buster and doing really teeny-weeny, small steps so it takes ages to walk to the wall.

"Come on, Gatesy. Hurry up."

"I can't walk fast - my shoes pinch," I tell him.

"OK, jump on then."

Before I know it, Buster is giving me a piggyback.

He runs right over to the wall by the school gates.

"No more excuses! You draw, I'll stand behind and cover for you."

Buster is serious.

Next, I start drawing slowly to waste more time.

"I know what you're up to – and I'm SURE Mr Keen would LOVE to read this,"

he says, starting to wave my **comic** around.

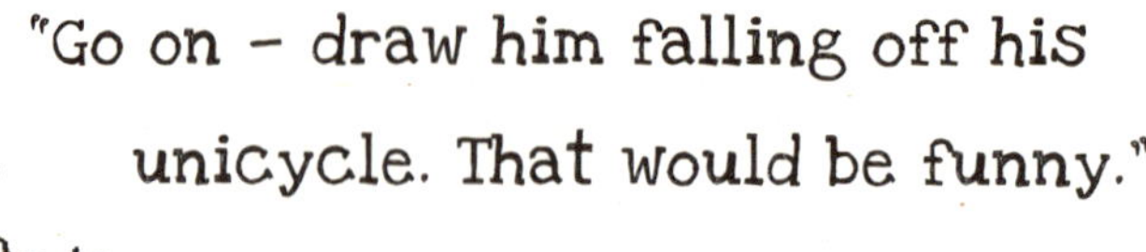

"Go on – draw him falling off his unicycle. That would be funny."

Buster is enjoying this a bit too much.

"I can't..." I tell him.

"YES you can, Gatesy, if you want your comic back."

"No, I really can't..." I say, because

Mr Fullerman is standing RIGHT BEHIND **Buster**.

"What's going on here? Tom, you weren't DRAWING on school property again, were you?"

"YES, he was, Sir – I was trying to stop him,"

Buster says before I can reply.

"Hey! That's not true!"

"What's that in your hand then?"

Buster asks, and POINTS to the **chalk.**

"Chalk, but..."

"I rest my case..."

Buster smiles at Mr Fullerman.

"He's got my **comic**, sir, and won't give it back!" I say.

"I have – it's all about Mr Keen and how he fell off his unicycle and didn't really HAVE a PROPER SPORTS injury at all."

"I'll take that comic, Buster, and there's to be no more drawing on walls by either of you," Mr Fullerman tells us. **Buster** winks at me and goes into school like nothing has happened.

Mr Fullerman starts to look through my **comic.**

"Did you draw this, Tom?"

"Yes, sir, but Miss Jam confiscated it from me because I was drawing in class."

"That's fair enough, Tom."

Then **Buster** got hold of it SOMEHOW, and told me unless I drew on the wall, he'd show it to Mr Keen.

"And why would that have been a bad thing?"

Because we were told he had a SPORTS INJURY and I've drawn the truth: that he fell off an out-of-control **unicycle!**

Mr Fullerman is looking at my **comic** and trying not to laugh.

"Oh, NOW I see."

THEN I lost the note that Mum gave me to explain what happened to Miss Jam's childhood toy, **Rodney Rat**.

"That's Miss Jam's toy?" Mr Fullerman repeats.

Yes – it wasn't my fault Rooster took him and threw him on top of Mr Akedo's car. We're still looking for him, so Granny knitted a NEW **Rodney** but that didn't work out so well.

I take a breath.

"I understand your stress, Tom.

I'll keep hold of your comic for now.

And I won't show it to Mr Keen."

That's a RELIEF.

"It's very funny. I like the bit where Mr Keen goes haring off outside – hilarious,"

Mr Fullerman adds.

"Thanks, sir. I do my best."

I go back to class, feeling like ONE problem is SOLVED.

Then I remember my drawing of **Rodney Rat.**

I'm expecting the worst.

AMY sits down next to me.

"Did **Buster** find you?" she asks.

"YES, and he STOLE my **comic** from Miss Jam's drawer. Mr Fullerman's got it now."

"How did **Buster** do that?"

"Who knows? He's sneaky."

"I've got my extra stars for helping Miss Jam," AMY says happily.

"NO stars for me once Miss Jam sees what happened to **Rodney.** It's only a matter of time," I sigh.

Miss Jam opens the red box file and takes out the worksheets.

My drawing is IN there somewhere.

She starts from the BACK of the classroom to hand them out.

When Miss Jam gets to me, I'm waiting for her to say something like:

How could you, Tom? POOR **Rodney Rat**! I'm SO disappointed...

She hands me my worksheet and says...

NOTHING.

I'm in **shock!**

I've even got three merits and a smiley face for my maths!

AMY nudges me.

"Here, take this, Tom, and DON'T lose it again."

Then under the table she passes me the

drawing of **Rodney Rat**!

I'm in **DOUBLE SHOCK.**

"HOW did you get that back?"

"I sneaked it out of the box while I was being Miss Jam's helper," she tells me.

AMY is a ☆ **HERO!** ☆

I want to CHEER and SHOUT "HOORAY!"

But I say "thank you" and high-five her instead.

Then Marcus nudges me on the other side.

"Hey, Tom, Derek's outside waving at you. Why isn't he in his class?"

I wave back, happy to see him.

"He's been to the dentist," I say.

Derek's holding something up at the door that I recognize.

I shout out at the TOP of my voice:

The whole class looks at Derek, who opens the door and comes in holding **Rodney Rat** proudly like he's a PRIZE.

Miss Jam JUMPS for JOY!

Then she looks **Rodney** over, checking that he's OK.

"Rodney's back!"

"Sorry, Miss Jam. Tom left **Rodney** at my house. But here he is, all safe and sound!" Derek says.

It's not the WHOLE story, but that doesn't matter...

Miss Jam is HAPPY and so am I.

"Miss, does this mean FRIDAY **PIE DAY** is back on?" I ask hopefully.

(It's a good question.)

Miss Jam thinks for a moment.

"We'll just have to see..."

FRIDAY **PIE DAY** FRIDAY **PIE DAY**

FRIDAY **PIE DAY** FRIDAY **PIE DAY**

Lack of pies means FRIDAY **PIE DAY** isn't happening today.

It's the weekend and there's LOTS of things to look forward to.

Things like:

Band practice with Norman, Leroy and Derek:

Playing with Rooster:

Hanging out with Delia:

The family get-together:

MONDAY:

I'm rushing around the house looking for my **comic**, but I can't find it  ANYWHERE!

"Don't forget your packed lunch, Tom... It's delicious," Delia tells me, and passes it over.

"You'd better not have eaten my biscuits!" I say, and she just shrugs.

"That's the sort of thing Mum does, not me," Delia says.

Mum comes in and she's holding my **comic** in her hand.

"Is THIS what you're looking for, Tom?"

"YES, that's it! Thanks, Mum!"

Mum gives me a LOOK.

"It's an interesting story, Tom – 'ANTS IN PANTS and the Chocolate Spread Thief', who I found very FAMILIAR."

"I don't know what you mean.

It's just Ants in Pants, Mum – that's all."

"In my defence, I didn't know it was YOUR chocolate spread, Delia..."

Mum tries to explain.

"Rita!" Dad pretends to be shocked.

"Don't start - you finish off the chocolate spread all the time!" Mum says.

"Told you it was Mum..." I tell Delia.

Mum hands me back my **comic**.

"Don't put EVERYTHING we do in a **comic**, will you, Tom?"

"As if I'd do that!" I say.

"I saw Mr Akedo yesterday too," Mum says with a LAUGH. "He had a lovely mini break and he thought people were being friendly and waving at him, not pointing at **Rodney Rat** on his roof!" says Mum.

I'm SO glad that Miss Jam never found out what really happened to **Rodney Rat**, and hopefully never will.

Back in class, Mr Fullerman is welcoming us in and being VERY jolly. He's made a few changes to the classroom. The first one is: his name is back on the door.

Mr Fullerman Class 5F

And there's a new poster on display, saying: Read with Robbie Rat.

(Everyone LOVES Robbie.)

READ with ROBBIE RAT

Pictures of where we READ:

Best of all, once a month at the end of the school day we get to have ... Monday Bun Day!

The whole class is very excited about that! It's going to make Mondays a lot more fun – and MONDAY **BUN DAY** makes for a very good chant as well.

MONDAY **BUN DAY** MONDAY **BUN DAY**

Mr Keen is enjoying taking our assembly and tells us how PLEASED he is to have recovered from his ...

We're trying hard not to LAUGH - but not as hard as the teachers. Mr Fullerman's shoulders are shaking a lot.

I got my **comic** back from Mr Fullerman, but only after all the teachers looked through it in the staffroom.

But best, BEST of all: Mr Keen says that Caretaker Stan has allowed us a section of the playground wall to DRAW on in chalk. He knows how popular that was. It's going to be the official

It's the FIRST thing we all want to do at break time.

Tina's already there. (Of course she is.)

Brilliant – I've got no chance of drawing now. She'll take up the WHOLE wall in no time.

But Tina says ...

"Hi, Tom! Can you show me how to draw one of your **MONSTERS?** The ANTS IN PANTS **comic** is HILARIOUS. I love your doodles!"

Which is a surprise.

"Thanks, Tina – I do my best," I say, and start drawing **MONSTERS.** It's going well, when **Buster Jones** turns up.

"THERE you are, Gatesy! Show me how to draw one of those monsters," he says – and of course I do.

It keeps him out of trouble (for now).

I'm busy doodling when Derek SPOTS something on the ground that looks like a book.

He picks it up and shows it to me.

"LOOK! It's Marcus's JOURNAL – the one he's been writing in secretly all this time and LAUGHING at," Derek tells me.

"I wonder what's in it..." I say.

"FUNNY stories about US, remember? He's been making his own **comic**. We should have a look," Derek says.

"We should!" I agree with him.

"Go on then..." Derek passes it to me.

"You first..." I tell Derek.

Eventually we open it together.

And we get a surprise...

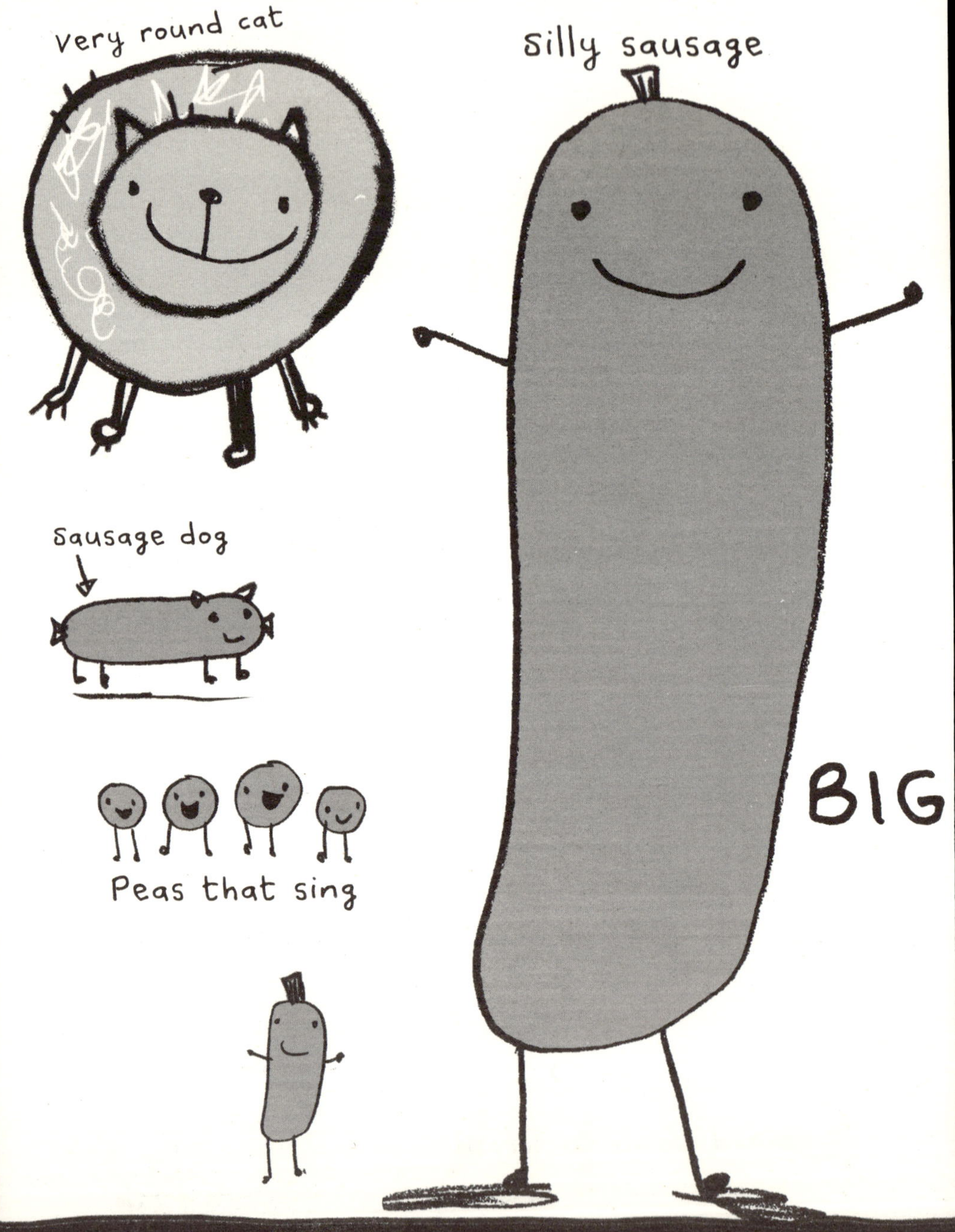
very round cat
silly sausage
sausage dog
Peas that sing
BIG

Miss Jam
Miss Jam's Jam
Flea
Ha!
Ha!
Ha!
Things that ☺ make me go Ha Ha
Funny line
by Marcus Meldrew
Big fluff
Small fluff
Me
being hilarious
Tom is funny.
Boo!
Derek makes me laugh.

This journal isn't what we were expecting.

Turns out I'm not the only one who is

Ha! Ha! HILARIOUS.

Read with Robbie Rat

(formerly known as **Rough Rodney**)

Your very own Robbie Rat, who will stare at you while you read your favourite book. ENJOY!

ANTS IN PANTS
Chocolate Spread Thief
Yummy!
Choco Spread
Yippee!
Choco Spread
Choco Spread
I love chocolate spread.
It's THE BEST
It's all gone!
Choco Spread
Grumpy Ant is coming!

It's empty!
Oh no!
I'm SHOCKED!
Are you REALLY?
Yes!
Did YOU eat my chocolate spread?
I don't like chocolate spread.
You do! I can tell.
How?
The spoon covered in chocolate spread.
Oh... that.
Choco Spread

THE ONE NOTE SONG

This is a
One note
One note
One note song

This is a
One note
One note
One note song
When you play one note
you can't go wrong

With a one note
One note
One note song

One note's
easier to sing
Spend less time
on practising

How many notes
can you play?
ONE
How many notes
can you say?
ONE
How many songs
have one note?
ONE
This is a
One note
One note
One note song

(Repeat chorus more
than once.)

How to draw ANTS IN PANTS

Different pants

The Ultimate book for Tom Gates fans to read and fill in all year round!

Packed with brand-new activities, makes and stories, and much, much more.

Look out for the NEXT

LAUGH-OUT-LOUD TOM GATES book from Liz Pichon

COMING IN OCTOBER 2025

Learn to draw with Liz!

Tips and tricks and a step-by-step guide to doodle in the Tom Gates style.

The must-have art activity book for fans of Tom Gates.

With SONGS from the award-winning TV SHOW!

Tom Gates music app that's FREE to download.

From DOGZOMBIES to DUDE3, music is a HUGE part of the Tom Gates world. Learn how to play all your favourite songs from the series with REAL notation for:

- Guitar
- Piano
- Ukulele
- Recorder

And with notation for drums and tips and tricks for vocals!

Read all the brilliant TOM GATES BOOKS!

TOM GATES
WHAT monster?
BY LIZ PICHON
TOM GATES
TEN TREMENDOUS TALES
HELLO
BY LIZ PICHON
TOM GATES
SPECTACULAR SCHOOL TRIP (Really...)
TOM GATES
RANDOM ACTS OF FUN
TOM GATES
HAPPY TO HELP
TOM GATES
FIVE STAR STORIES
BY LIZ PICHON
THE TOM GATES MUSIC BOOK
TOM GATES
BIG BOOK OF FUN STUFF
BY LIZ PICHON
YOU CAN DRAW
TOM GATES
WITH LIZ PICHON
TOM GATES
MEGA MAKE AND DO AND STORIES TOO
TOM GATES
BOOK OF EVERYTHING
BY LIZ PICHON
TOM GATES
is HA! HA! HILARIOUS
TOM GATES
PESKY PETS AND PARTIES
BY LIZ PICHON
My name IS Strawberrie Jam!
For more fun stuff...
visit thebrilliantworldoftomgates.com

Read all the Tom Gates books?

Well, now you can read ***SHOE WARS***, a standalone adventure story.

A *Sunday Times* Children's Book of the Year pick.

"Bursting with imagination and fabulous gadgets, ***Shoe Wars*** is full of Pichon's characteristic warmth, humour and quirky illustrations"
The Bookseller

"A tale oozing creativity and packed with pen and ink illustrations, exciting and expressive typography and visual jokes" *BookTrust*

Welcome to Shoe Town – and meet Ruby and Bear Foot. They are running out of time to rescue their inventor dad from his hideous boss, Wendy Wedge. She'll do ANYTHING to win the glitzy Golden Shoe Award and knows that entering flying shoes is her hot ticket to the trophy. Flying shoes that Ruby and Bear just happen to be hiding...

Liz Pichon is one of the UK's best-loved and bestselling creators of children's books. Her TOM GATES series has been translated into 45 languages, sold millions of copies worldwide, and has won the Roald Dahl Funny Prize, the Blue Peter Book Award for Best Story and the younger fiction category of the Waterstones Children's Book Prize. The TOM GATES books have inspired the nation's children to get creative, whether that's through reading, drawing, doodling, writing, making music or performing.

"I wanted to FILL the books with ALL the things I loved doing when I was a kid. It's just the best feeling ever to know children are enjoying reading the books, because I love making them. So thank you so much for choosing Tom Gates and keep reading and doodling!"

(School photo of Liz being grump

Visit Liz at www.lizpichon.com